"All history is gossip."

—PRESIDENT JOHN F. KENNEDY

Uncle Sam, whose image represents the United States

Lives

OF THE

Presidents

FAME, SHAME

(and What the Neighbors Thought)

WRITTEN BY KATHLEEN KRULL

ILLUSTRATED BY KATHRYN HEWITT

SCHOLASTIC INC.

New York Toronto London Auckland Sydney
Mexico City New Delhi Hong Kong

We are indebted to Helen Foster James, Ed Heffernan, Emily Schell of the
San Diego Office of Education, Paul Hewitt, Dave Hewitt, Rubin Pfeffer, Jeannette Larson,
Vicky Reed and her class at the University of San Diego, and the fourth- and fifth-grade
teachers at Grant Elementary School in Santa Monica, California: Carol Timmerman,
Judy Adams, Nancy Ramsey, Jan Baird, Susan Croft, Carolyn Matsumura,
Paula Freimund, Jacque Savage, and JoAnne Ten Brink.
—K. K. and K. H.

ISBN 0-439-16830-9

12   5/0

Printed in the U.S.A.   14

First Scholastic printing, January 2000

The illustrations in this book were done
in watercolor and colored pencil on watercolor paper.
The title was hand lettered by Georgia Deaver.
The display type was set in Snell Roundhand and the text type was set in Goudy Old Style.
Design by Linda Lockowitz

For Marie Tollstrup, alias Sister Della,
my eighth-grade English teacher at St. Joseph's School
in Wilmette, Illinois
—K. K.

For Karen Delshad, Sylvia Anderle, Toni Mitchell,
and Louix Escobar, the inspiring librarians at the Fairview Library
in Santa Monica, California
—K. H.

Contents

Introduction

WE NAME SCHOOLS and streets after our presidents and put their heads on our money. We envision them as larger-than-life leaders and boast that in America any child can aspire to be one. But what were the presidents really like—as human beings? We know that (so far) all have been white men. Most were wealthy, well-educated, members of Protestant religions, middle-aged (though visibly older when they left office), and married to women who encouraged or even directed them. Sometimes they seem to blur together, a bland bunch of faceless, wartless heroes.

Not to their neighbors. Those close to the presidents knew how to see the details, like who had feet bigger than his ego (Washington), who barked like a seal (Kennedy), who hosted the neighborhood Halloween parties (Nixon), who dissected small animals (Madison), who could make the president eat food he didn't like (Franklin Roosevelt's housekeeper), and who always had to be "it" during hide-and-seek (Theodore Roosevelt). At least one president had actual warts (Lincoln), bribed dogs with candy-coated vitamins (Lyndon Johnson), dined on popcorn (Reagan), joked about dating mummies (Clinton), let mockingbirds eat from his own mouth (Jefferson), and fought watermelon-seed wars (Truman). As dangerous as it can be to be president—one in five has died on the job—it can be dangerously enlightening to be a neighbor to one. Each man has been, in fact, colorful and quirky in his own way.

Focusing on modern presidents and the most notable names from the past, this book looks at our leaders with a cool, contemporary eye, respectful but definitely nosy. Other books discuss these men in relation to great historical events, the context of their actions, their political achievements, and public opinion rankings. This book is about the lives of presidents as fathers, husbands, pet owners, and neighbors. These are stories about hairstyles, attitudes, diets, bad habits, ailments, fears, money, sleep patterns, and underwear. They are offered now in the hope of surprising even those who believe they know the presidents well.

—*Kathleen Krull*

George Washington

BORN IN WESTMORELAND COUNTY, VIRGINIA, 1732
DIED IN MOUNT VERNON, VIRGINIA, 1799

Revolutionary War hero
who defined a role of lasting importance
as the world's first elected president

AT SIX FEET TWO INCHES, George Washington had big muscles, big moves (always elegant and powerful), and big feet (size thirteen). He stood out, literally head and shoulders above ordinary people—he looked the way people thought a president should.

His look wasn't glamorous, with smallpox scars on his face and his mouth pushed out of shape by false teeth (made of materials like ivory, not wood as is commonly thought). Like many at the time, he felt that regular bathing was unhealthy, but he dressed fashionably and wore his military uniforms at every opportunity.

Washington had other things working against him besides bad teeth. He wasn't scholarly; he had the equivalent of an eighth-grade education. Insecure about preferring action to reading, he worried about manners and once copied by hand 110 rules about "Civility and Decent Behavior in Company and Conversation." He did subscribe to ten newspapers, and he did keep a diary, but it was mostly a record of what the women looked like at balls.

His ways with women weren't dashing. The mushy love poetry he wrote was unsuccessful until he met Martha Dandridge Custis, a wealthy widow with two children. Everyone who met her called her nice; he called her a "quiet wife" with a "quiet soul." More than a foot shorter than he was, she would pull on his lapels to bring his face close to hers when she wanted to talk to him.

He wasn't fatherly, though he was thought of that way. His size intimidated children, as did the rarity of his smile (partly this was to conceal his teeth, but also he felt that life was too serious for joking around). With no children of his own (he adopted Martha's), all evidence suggests that he was probably sterile.

In public he was a poor speaker unless he had a prepared speech. Noticeably reserved, with a motto of "Be courteous to all but intimate with few," he was not the kind of man you slapped on the back—someone did it once and immediately, seeing his startled face, regretted it. It was a point of pride for him to hide his feelings, and he often communicated by silence or frowns. He did have a temper and devoted much energy to controlling it.

He wasn't fiercely ambitious. After his war service he would have preferred life as a gentleman farmer at Mount Vernon, the estate he had inherited and the only place where he was really at ease. But overriding all was a desire to make himself useful to others; when he was asked to do something—like lead the country instead of retiring to his farm—he always followed through.

Modest and shy, he found fanfare embarrassing and would disappear if the praise grew too flowery. At the first reception in his honor, he was aghast to hear himself loudly announced as "The president of the United States!" (At future events he made sure he was already in the room when a reception started, casually leaning on the mantel so he wouldn't have to make a grand entrance.) He appeared openly awed by his duties, almost sad, acutely aware that everyone was watching everything he did. "I walk on untrodden ground," he fretted.

With no major scandal in his life, some thought him so pure as to be boring, or else chameleonlike, even hypocritical. But most were struck by his integrity. Influenced in part by his Episcopalian faith, he developed and stuck to a personal code of right and wrong. He went along with the custom of slavery, though he found it personally repugnant and hoped it would end. In his last twenty years he rarely bought a slave and found discreet ways to free some; in his will he freed the rest upon Martha's death.

People found other reasons to admire Washington besides integrity. He was rich, especially once he married Martha. As the country's first millionaire, he politely declined his presidential salary of $25,000. And he was an animal lover. Especially devoted to his faithful dogs, he gave them names like Sweetlips, Madame Moose, Vulcan, and True Love. He had grooms brush the teeth of his horses every morning.

But what really stood out about Washington was his sheer bravery. During the Revolutionary War, the British noticed that General Washington just would not give up or go away. Famous for taking daring risks and for superhuman stamina, he could stay awake for days at a stretch (even on horseback) and survive any ordeal, including walking through gunfire untouched. After the war, with Washington linked so closely to American independence, there simply was no other choice as leader: He is the only president who was elected unanimously.

Also the only president not to live in the White House (it hadn't been built yet), Washington lived in various executive mansions. Up at dawn, he shaved and had his hair combed, powdered if the occasion was formal, and tied back with a ribbon. Breakfast was three buttered cornmeal cakes smothered with honey, plus three cups of tea. Favorite dishes included crabmeat soup (one of Martha's specialties), sweet potatoes with coconut, ham with oyster sauce, and string beans with mushrooms. He usually went to bed early, but if visitors had interesting news or if Washington particularly liked them, he would stay up to linger over champagne.

When he finally returned to his beloved Mount Vernon after his presidency, he expanded the farm from twenty-five hundred acres to eight thousand, gradually taking over the neighborhood. "The General and I feel like children just released from school," Martha confided to a friend—but the horde of visitors continued. Washington was such an excellent host that he'd bring hot tea to your room at night if he heard you coughing.

One snowy morning when he was sixty-seven, he took his usual horseback ride around his property and soon afterward fell ill. Diagnosed with acute tonsillitis or pneumonia, he apologized for causing trouble and tried to make those near him less afraid of what would come. "It is well, I die hard, but I am not afraid to go" were his reported last words. Ever conscious of dignity, he had requested a simple burial. But he got a spectacle anyway, complete with gun salute.

John Adams

BORN IN 1735 AND DIED IN 1826
IN QUINCY, MASSACHUSETTS

Leading Boston lawyer, diplomat,
first vice president, second president,
and shaper of early America

"HE MEANS WELL," Benjamin Franklin said grudgingly of his fellow statesman John Adams. Others found Adams conceited, tactless, stubborn, and ridiculously petty—almost a comic figure.

Once people got to know him he seemed merely a pale and pudgy curmudgeon. But he made a truly pompous first impression. Ill at ease even with close acquaintances, he was very uncomfortable around strangers—he wouldn't make small talk, refused to flatter people, and detested off-color jokes. His reputation for pretentiousness was not helped when he said things like "There are few people in this world with whom I can converse." Even he was aware of his faults—he described himself as "obnoxious and unpopular."

Always paranoid, he believed the unpopularity was a plot and that he was cursed by being short. But his height was average and the real curse was his temper—so volcanic that Franklin called him "absolutely out of his senses." He thought of himself as "tranquil" but had a long list of things that made him lose control. He often gave people the silent treatment and let jealousy ripen into passionate bitterness.

Perhaps to make up for his personality problems, Adams worked harder than anyone else. Up at four o'clock every morning, he was in motion until ten o'clock each night—engaging in constant travel, meetings, and the reading and writing of documents. Occasionally he socialized over dinner and cigars, but he felt guilty if he did anything besides work. He lived frugally, was not interested in science or any arts (he particularly hated landscape paintings), and he made little time for family or fun.

He once said that he doubted he would have been a success without his wife at his side—though technically they were seldom next to each other. Adams met Abigail Smith while he was recovering from being jilted by another woman, but within a short time he was calling Abigail "Miss Adorable" and praising her "fair complexion, her crimson blushes, and her million charms and graces." One of the best-educated women in the colonies, Abigail took care of the modest Adams family farm while her husband was away on business, raised four children (including a future president) mostly alone, and influenced American politics by way of up to three letters a day to her husband. "Remember the ladies," she urged in some of the most famous words in the history of women's rights, "and be more generous and favorable to them than your ancestors!" Adams had some advanced ideas about women—he thought they were "better than men in general" and he considered his marriage an equal partnership—but the whole subject was taken so lightly in those days that his answer to his wife was to laugh at her for being "so saucy."

In some ways, Adams's arrogance camouflaged a gentle nature. With his family he could be warm and compassionate, often hosting relatives in need. Rarely did he and Abigail argue or even disagree (except over his many absences—she often referred to herself as a "widow" and even brought up the extremely rare subject of divorce). They both thought slavery was immoral and refused to have slaves, though they could have afforded them.

Although he had the longest life of any president, Adams had more than his share of maladies. He caught cold at any draft and was plagued with chest pains, boils, spells of depression and despair, and chronically red, watery eyes. He blushed easily, especially when shocked (as when a woman seated next to him at one dinner brought up the facts of life). Missing most teeth, he refused to wear false ones, so talked with a lisp. He began his lifelong habit of smoking at age eight. Enemies named him "His Rotundity," and even Abigail called him "so very fat."

The first residents of what came to be called the White House—so remote that, on the way there, they got lost several times in the woods—the Adamses found life as the First Family cold, damp, and unhealthy. Wet plaster oozed from the walls, bathrooms were outdoors, firewood was hard to come by, and the main source of water was at a park five blocks away. Abigail found the place a "splendid misery," but she did see more of her husband once he became president, sometimes for a breakfast or dinner together. Mostly he stayed in his office, while she supervised the large staff and found ways to obtain their favorite New England foods: cider, white potatoes, cranberries, hams, and a type of pudding called Floating Island.

Adams had stables built, in which he kept his favorite horse, Cleopatra. He tried to find time to ride daily—he liked the way it set his "blood in motion." His main hobby was reading—"You will never be alone with a poet in your pocket," he said—and he kept a diary of people, places, and events. On travels he collected souvenirs—and sometimes stole them, as when he took a sliver of wood from a chair at William Shakespeare's birthplace. He and Abigail tended to be intolerant of other religions besides Unitarianism, and they advocated press censorship—especially after a newspaper referred to him as "old querulous bald blind crippled toothless Adams."

From the Chair of Wm. Shakespeare

Reading books "whirled away the time" during his long retirement, until cataracts made reading hard and he had one of his eleven grandchildren read aloud to him. At age eighty-nine, he became the only president to get the thrill of seeing his son elected president—his favorite, John Quincy. He was nearly overcome with pride that was magnified by disappointment (in his underachieving other children) and glee (surely his son's victory vindicated his own accomplishments).

The following year, he grew steadily weaker but attained his goal of surviving until the fiftieth anniversary of the signing of the Declaration of Independence. When asked for words to celebrate that special Fourth of July, he said, "Independence forever!" He died later that day, of heart failure and pneumonia.

Thomas Jefferson

BORN IN ALBEMARLE COUNTY, VIRGINIA, 1743
DIED IN MONTICELLO, VIRGINIA, 1826

Helped to define America
as the author of the Declaration of Independence,
secretary of state, vice president, and president

THE GAWKY YOUNG MAN with all those freckles set his own timetable for study: agriculture, botany, zoology, chemistry, anatomy, and religion from five o'clock to eight o'clock in the morning; law and politics from eight o'clock to one o'clock; history in the afternoons (with time out for a two-mile run in the country); literature, languages, and oratory each night.

Thomas Jefferson matured into an unusually well-read lawyer—and our most versatile president. Everything interested him, from traveling by balloon to playing violin (which he did for as much as three hours a day), from gardening and nature (his idea of a great time was tasting fresh asparagus, smelling the lilacs in bloom, and seeing the first whippoorwill of the season) to architecture (he designed one of the most beautiful homes in America—Monticello, his palatial mountaintop estate).

He wanted to include his wife, Martha Wayles Skelton, known as Patty, in all he did. But seven pregnancies in ten years weakened her, and her death at age thirty-three devastated him. Immersing himself in politics was his way of getting over the loss, as was lavishing attention on his two surviving daughters (and later his eleven grandchildren, thanks to whom Jefferson has more living descendants than any other president).

As committed as he was to public service, Jefferson considered Monticello his life's work. It was where he collected books (ultimately sixty-five hundred—the most impressive library in America at the time), experimented with exotic crops (Italian wine grapes, garlic, oranges, rice, and marijuana for use as hemp in making clothes), invented numerous labor-saving devices (the swivel chair, an adjustable table, beds that retracted into the walls), and threw gourmet dinner parties with beef, Italian macaroni, french fries, and the latest dessert sensation—ice cream wrapped in pastry crust. He often spent the large sum of $50 a day on groceries; his wine bill during eight years as president was more than $10,000.

Jefferson's most significant achievement as president was the Louisiana Purchase, which doubled the size of the United States—enlarging the "neighborhood." He also tried to expand his own neighborhood by having his friends construct estates around Monticello, even paving roads between his property and theirs. He wielded his masterful pen to create yet another neighborhood—one of the mind. He wrote more than eighteen thousand letters, and just the record he kept of mail going in and out ran to 656 pages. "Nothing is more important," he felt, "than to acquire a facility of developing our ideas on paper."

Some American clergy condemned Jefferson as an "atheist," and opponents liked to scream that "murder, robbery, rape, adultery, and incest will be openly taught and practiced" under him as president. It was true that Jefferson belonged to no church, but he contributed money to several, attended services occasionally, and championed religious freedom.

Author of the most famous defense of fundamental human rights in the world—the Declaration of Independence—Jefferson was also a man of his times. He disliked women who influenced their husbands' politics, educated his daughters to defer to men, and advised one daughter against neglecting to wear her bonnet in the sun "because it will make you very ugly and then we should not love you so much." Privately he was tormented by the concept of slavery, but he was economically dependent on his 120 slaves and wasn't willing to give them up.

Historians disagree violently about Jefferson's possible affair with a slave, Sally Hemings. Some argue that their relationship lasted thirty-eight years and produced several children; others remain convinced that this would have been totally out of character for Jefferson. Jefferson himself offered no evidence either way.

He enjoyed the company of women, and they treasured him as gentle, sweet, a good listener who made them feel at ease, and someone they could depend on for favors. Some people found him cold and reserved, almost sanctimonious, but this impression was really due to his shyness. His low, soft voice was effective for conversation, but he was unable to raise it and tended to mumble when speaking in public. He prized self-control (he lost his temper only twice, according to one daughter) and didn't show emotion, giving him what one observer called "a rambling, vacant look." His posture was poor and his style casual—he dressed for comfort, not fashion, and liked his farmer clothes the best even if they were a little small on him. Some found it shocking that he might be wearing his muddy riding boots when ladies called, or that he greeted foreign officials while in worn slippers and sloppy clothes, but many found his unpretentious ways refreshing. Basically healthy (he bathed his feet daily in icy cold water in the belief that this prevented colds), he distrusted doctors and saw one only when necessary.

He believed in rights for animals and sheltered peacocks, partridges, and grizzly bears (in cages, though sometimes allowed out to stroll around the garden). He let pet mockingbirds fly around free, eat from his own mouth, and serenade him during his afternoon naps. He filled his pockets with corn to feed to his tame deer.

At the end of his presidency, exhausted from public service and bogged down in grief for lost loved ones, Jefferson couldn't wait to retire to Monticello to devote himself to farming, books, and the grandchildren who bunked in the estate's distinctive dome. He rode horseback daily until the year he died, at age eighty-three, probably of prostate problems. In a bizarre presidential coincidence, he died on the same day as John Adams—the fiftieth anniversary of the Declaration of Independence. "Is it the Fourth?" were his last words.

Jefferson left Monticello to a daughter. But his gracious lifestyle had always been a bit beyond his means, and the estate was sold to cover his debts.

James Madison

BORN IN PORT CONWAY, VIRGINIA, 1751
DIED AT MONTPELIER, VIRGINIA, 1836

*Congressman and president known as
"Father of the Constitution" for his role
in shaping the American form of government*

FRIENDS TEASED HIM for being "no bigger than a half piece of soap." Enemies called him "Little Pygmy," and even his wife referred to him as her "darling little husband."

Our tiniest president, James Madison weighed only one hundred pounds. Sickly, nervous, and shy, he looked like a boy until he was well into his thirties. His voice was so low and weak that he often could not be heard at all. Awkward at parties, he was ridiculed as "the most unsociable creature in existence" and was once described as always looking like he was on his way to a funeral. He delayed decisions as long as possible, which made him seem uncertain.

But neighbors and everyone else noticed that Madison was always the best-informed person in any situation. He completed college at what is now Princeton in two years, where he had a reputation for never saying or doing anything improper. He was the only one smart enough to take notes when the Constitution was written, giving us our only record of the process. After drafting the Bill of Rights, he made it his business to get it added to the Constitution. An Episcopalian but not particularly devout, he was admired for his integrity and his knowledge of human nature—"If men were angels, no government would be necessary," he observed.

Powdering his hair white, he pulled it back to make himself appear older. He dressed in serious black, always neatly, and was the first president to wear long pants (the others wore short ones, or knickers). Aware of his reputation for timidity, he cultivated his stubborn side and came to be known as "obstinate as a mule." He had at least one un-timid hobby—considering himself an amateur scientist, he liked to dissect rabbits and other small animals.

And although he waited until he was forty-three to find it, he had a secret weapon—Dolley Payne Todd. Once he married her, he could stand back, the amiable husband letting his perky, outgoing wife get all the attention. A legendary hostess, trendsetter, and matchmaker, Dolley genuinely loved people and soon became the most popular person in America. She wore emeralds, ostrich-feathered turbans, robes of pink satin trimmed with ermine, and heavy rouge and other cosmetics normally judged as immoral, but not in her case. (More shocking to some was her habit of using snuff in public.) She had strong opinions and acted as trusted adviser to Madison, but believed that "Politics is the business of men . . . I care only about *people*." People all over wanted to know what she was serving for dinner. The Madisons liked champagne ("most delightful," he said), chocolate, and expensive imported treats. They had no children, but enjoyed Madison's more than thirty nieces and nephews.

Madison owned lots of land, but poor yields on tobacco and wheat gave him little income. Though he hated the system of slavery, he agreed with those who thought abolition was secondary to a strong America. He had slaves but helped organize a society that founded Liberia in West Africa as a colony for freed slaves.

The man once called "a gloomy stiff creature" became much more playful and full of jokes once he retired to Montpelier, his five-thousand-acre plantation overlooking the Blue Ridge Mountains. When he became too frail for his daily horseback rides, he would sit on the porch and tell stories about famous people he had known, while visitors listened, drank coffee, and smoked cigars. At witty remarks (from himself or others), his bright blue eyes "would twinkle wickedly," according to one guest.

With more stamina than he appeared to have, Madison lasted until age eighty-five, when his heart failed. His last words—after a niece asked him what was the matter—were "Nothing more than a change of *mind*, my dear." After his death Dolley returned to Washington and lived another thirteen years, more popular than ever.

James Monroe

BORN IN WESTMORELAND COUNTY, VIRGINIA, 1758
DIED IN NEW YORK CITY, 1831

NEIGHBORS DEEMED the man who gave his name to the Monroe Doctrine (warning Europe against expansion in America) a bit dull; he could be warm, but his feelings seemed bottled up. He was well groomed but not fashionable. The first president to tour the country, he was also the first to regularly display his own hair in public (previous presidents usually wore wigs). An Episcopalian, he opposed slavery. His wife, Elizabeth, preferred to avoid "boorish" Washington society; her unpopularity increased when she restricted the guest list to a mere thirty at the wedding of their daughter Maria, the first First Child to marry in the White House. Monroe died of heart failure at age seventy-three—the third president to die on Independence Day.

John Quincy Adams

BORN IN QUINCY, MASSACHUSETTS, 1767
DIED IN WASHINGTON, D.C., 1848

"I AM CERTAINLY not intentionally repulsive," wrote the only son of a president to become president. But like his father, he was one of the prickliest and least liked. He wore the same hat for ten years (neighbors complained). Sometimes his parties were boycotted, so he and his wife, Louisa, a singer and harpist, spent many hostile evenings alone. They had three sons and one daughter (out of a total of nineteen pregnancies in twenty-one years) and disagreed about child care and most everything else. Although he believed that enjoyment was a sign of weakness, Adams installed the first pool table in the White House, kept an alligator as a pet, and jumped into the icy Potomac River for a swim almost every morning of his life—in the nude. Going on after his presidency to serve in Congress for seventeen years, Adams collapsed there while making an antislavery speech, dying of a stroke at age eighty.

Andrew Jackson

BORN IN WAXHAW, SOUTH CAROLINA, 1767
DIED NEAR NASHVILLE, TENNESSEE, 1845

*Lawyer, greatest military hero
of his day, and the "people's president"—
the first whose origins were humble*

PEOPLE HE'D GROWN UP WITH went into shock when they heard the news of the election: "Well, if Andrew Jackson can become president," said one former neighbor, "anybody can!"

Ex-presidents feared him as "dangerous" and "a barbarian." They knew how Jackson had spent his youth: fighting (especially with anyone who made fun of his childhood drooling), partying, gambling, and playing practical jokes (like relocating outhouses to far-off places). But once he married Rachel Donelson Robards, the daughter of his landlady, he became more focused and considerate. And after he emerged—nicknamed "Old Hickory" for his toughness—from the stunning victory over the British at the Battle of New Orleans, he was wildly popular among ordinary Americans.

Jackson actually married Rachel twice, because her divorce from her abusive first husband hadn't been finalized in time for the first wedding to be legal. His opponents kept bringing this story up, during the first vicious campaign in presidential history. When Rachel went shopping for clothes to wear as First Lady, she happened to see a campaign pamphlet and learned of the lurid attacks against her, with mentions of bigamy and adultery. Deeply religious, she became hysterical at the accusations of sin and died within the month of an apparent heart attack, three months before Jackson was even inaugurated.

So she missed the famous riot at his inaugural party, when unexpected crowds fought over barrels of orange punch, smashed china and glasses, tracked mud over

White House furniture, and almost suffocated Jackson. He fled to dine with friends on sirloin from a prize ox and spent his first night as president at a hotel.

Jackson grieved for Rachel the rest of his life, dressing in a black suit and tie, black armband, and black band around his tall beaver hat. A tiny picture of her hung on a black cord next to his heart; he read from her prayer book every night. They had no children, but he adopted his wife's nephew and raised several other children whose parents could not take care of them. They included an Indian boy, Lyncoya, whose family was killed during a war with the Creek Indians. Jackson had some 160 slaves, including some he brought to the White House with him, and he believed that slavery was not a matter for government action.

Assumed to be the president most likely to die in office (although he didn't), Jackson was in almost constant pain, racked with headaches, stomachaches, and a hacking cough. By the time he took office, his red hair had gone gray (and sometimes appeared to stand up as though at attention). A man who aroused passions, he was the first president to be the victim of an assassination attempt, the only president ever to kill a man in a duel (fought over Rachel's honor), and the only president to have been a prisoner of war (during the American Revolution).

Besides his numerous scars, Jackson lived with two bullets inside him—one he eventually had removed, with no anesthesia, after twenty years; the other remained near his heart and caused him pain all his life. Generally he obeyed doctors' orders, as long as they didn't tell him to give up coffee or tobacco. When he felt too ill for activity, he used the time for thinking; sometimes he spent entire days in bed.

Once the inauguration fiasco was behind him, Jackson brought improvements to the White House. He added running water and fully equipped bathrooms, a formal garden, a hothouse full of plants, and a $300 piano. He had "frolics" for the many children he knew, with blindman's bluff and snowball fights with cotton balls. Not a big eater himself (he picked at his food), he gave sumptuous candlelight dinners, with six kinds of wine, wild turkey dressed with brains, chicken served with slices of tongue, duck with celery, partridge with sweetbreads, pheasant, and Virginia ham— and for dessert, small Turkish tarts. He preferred to sit not at the head of the table, but between two women with whom he could be playful but dignified, a good listener but not a gossip, and an animated conversationalist. He sometimes mispronounced or misused words (and he never got the hang of spelling).

He insisted that the White House belonged to the people and that anyone should be able to walk in at any hour and shake the president's hand. Of course, that meant sometimes they'd see him in old clothes, feet on the desk, smoking his favorite corn-cob pipe. Breeding and racing horses—Bolivia, Emily, Lady Nashville, and others—were his favorite amusements, followed by raising birds and entering them in cock-fights. His parrot, named Poll, somehow knew many swear words.

To friends, Jackson was always loyal and generous; to enemies (especially anyone he held responsible for the rumors against Rachel), he was mean and spiteful. The shrieking high pitch of his voice could make him sound out of control, but his de-liberate way of turning his temper on and off amazed observers—he used the tech-nique to scare people into doing what he wanted. His thin-skinned, combative ways came in handy, as when his would-be assassin (a mentally disturbed house painter) shot at him; quick-thinking Jackson immediately jumped forward and hit the man with the cane he used to steady his walk.

His last years at the Hermitage, his large plantation, were uncomfortable. He had one functioning lung and one blind eye, and after his nightly visits to Rachel's grave site, he went to sleep propped up. The bad market for cotton forced him to borrow money from friends. Late in life he formally joined the Presbyterian Church and read many religious books. His dying wish was that he would meet friends—"both black and white," he emphasized—on the other side. His last words were "Oh, do not cry. Be good children, and we shall all meet in Heaven." He died at age seventy-eight, probably of heart failure, and was buried next to Rachel in the Hermitage garden.

Martin Van Buren

BORN IN 1782 AND DIED IN 1862
IN KINDERHOOK, NEW YORK

THE FIRST PRESIDENT born an American citizen (previous presidents started out as British subjects) spoke Dutch at home. Van Buren was also the first to campaign like a contemporary politician—with speeches, rallies, sing-alongs, and fundraisers. After his wife, Hannah (with whom he had four sons), died at age thirty-five, he never remarried. He was quick to laugh, enjoyed opera and theater, and dressed so impeccably that some scorned him as pretentious. An enthusiastic singer, he drowned out the neighbors during hymns at Episcopal services. He fought to keep a gift of two tiger cubs for himself but eventually had to turn them over to the zoo. Van Buren retired to Lindenwald, his farm, where he grew potatoes, fished, and plotted a political comeback that never occurred. He died of heart failure at age seventy-nine.

William Henry Harrison

BORN IN CHARLES CITY COUNTY, VIRGINIA, 1773
DIED IN WASHINGTON, D.C., 1841

THE OLDEST MAN to become president so far (at age sixty-eight), Harrison did the family shopping. The last purchases of his life were a Bible and a new cow, Sukey. Once elected, he insisted on giving the longest inauguration speech in history, on a frosty day, without overcoat, hat, or gloves. He got a cold, then pneumonia, and said, "I am ill, very ill, much more so than they think me." He died after only one month in office—the president with the shortest term, the only one who had studied to become a doctor, and the only one to have a grandson become president. Anna, the oldest First Lady thus far (at age sixty-five) and the first with a formal education, taught their ten children as well as many of the neighbors'. She experienced many tragedies—outliving Harrison and all but one of her children.

John Tyler

BORN IN CHARLES CITY COUNTY, VIRGINIA, 1790
DIED IN RICHMOND, VIRGINIA, 1862

THE PRESIDENT WITH the most children, Tyler said he loved having "a houseful of goodly babies budding around me." He was playing marbles with his boys when he found out he'd won the presidential election. With Letitia, his first wife, he had eight children. After her death, Tyler sparked much gossip among the neighbors by marrying Julia, who was younger than three of his daughters; he and Julia had seven babies. The Tylers gave some of the most energetic White House parties ever, introduced the previously forbidden polka, and kept guests entertained with his violin playing and her singing. Tyler, who was pro-slavery, retired to Sherwood Forest, his Virginia plantation. He died there at age seventy-one of bronchitis, a year and a half after his last child was born.

James K. Polk

BORN IN MECKLENBURG COUNTY, NORTH CAROLINA, 1795
DIED IN NASHVILLE, TENNESSEE, 1849

THOUGH HE INSTITUTED "Hail to the Chief" as the accompaniment to a presidential entrance and hosted the first Thanksgiving dinner at the White House, Polk gave some of its most boring parties. No music, alcohol, or dancing were allowed; Polk himself was humorless and suspicious. His wife, Sarah, who was extremely religious, was his private secretary and his chief consultant. They had no children, worked hard, and slept little. Polk virtually worked himself to death, dying at age fifty-three, three months after leaving the White House—the shortest retirement of any president. Not trusting banks, he'd kept his money in bags around the house. He left everything to Sarah, with the provision that their slaves be freed at her death. She lived for forty-two more years, never leaving home again except to go to church.

Zachary Taylor

BORN IN ORANGE COUNTY, VIRGINIA, 1784
DIED IN WASHINGTON, D.C., 1850

TAYLOR CHEWED TOBACCO and was famous for never missing the spittoon. Also famous during the United States–Mexican War as a general—nicknamed "Old Rough and Ready"—he was the first president who had never held any previous political office. He wore odd combinations of civilian and military dress and was a terrible speller. His warhorse, Old Whitey, grazed on the White House lawn. He and his reclusive wife, Margaret, had six children; neighbors guessed she had promised God to give up society if Taylor returned safely from war. After sixteen months in office, he suffered a digestive upset from pickled cucumbers, cherries, and an iced milk. He died five days later at age sixty-five. He'd opposed slavery but believed it was a "necessary evil," and his estate included more than one hundred slaves.

Millard Fillmore

BORN IN CAYUGA COUNTY, NEW YORK, 1800
DIED IN BUFFALO, NEW YORK, 1874

WHENEVER HE RETURNED from trips, Fillmore had armloads of new books for Abigail, the first First Lady to have held a job outside the home. As a young teacher, she'd had nineteen-year-old Fillmore in her class (he missed school as a child, but by thirty was a prosperous lawyer). She quit teaching after having the first of their two children and went on to establish a library for First Families in the White House. In the kitchen, the Fillmores switched from an open fireplace to a stove, though none of them (including the cook) knew how to use it. Fillmore was the first president with a stepmother and had no known bad habits. After Abigail's death, he married Caroline, who signed a prenuptial agreement putting him in charge of her fortune. In their mansion, he suffered two strokes and died at age seventy-four.

Franklin Pierce

BORN IN HILLSBORO, NEW HAMPSHIRE, 1804
DIED IN CONCORD, MASSACHUSETTS, 1869

WITH A CASCADE OF dark curly hair, Pierce is generally hailed as the handsomest president. Hearty and outgoing, he loved late-night mingling, but he lacked self-confidence and was often depressed. A lifelong battle with alcoholism undermined his health, and his wife, Jane, was even more frail. The Pierces were crushed when each of their three sons died, the last in a freak accident: Eleven-year-old Bennie fell out of a runaway railroad car and was killed as his parents watched. White House life was bleak, though Pierce did install central heating, a much-needed second bathroom, and the first Christmas tree. Retirement was even bleaker, when New England friends and neighbors shunned him for his support of the South in the Civil War. He died at age sixty-four of an inflammation of the stomach.

James Buchanan

BORN NEAR MERCERSBURG, PENNSYLVANIA, 1791
DIED IN LANCASTER, PENNSYLVANIA, 1868

SHE CALLED HIM "NUNC," and he called her his "mischievous romp of a niece"—Harriet Lane hosted White House parties along with her uncle, the only president who never married. Buchanan had another politician as a roommate for so long (sixteen years) that they were thought of as a couple, yielding many rumors (but no evidence) that Buchanan was homosexual. People sent him pets for company, including a herd of elephants, a pair of bald eagles, and a Newfoundland dog. Nearsighted in one eye and farsighted in the other, Buchanan compensated by cocking his head to the left. He believed that slavery should be legal but bought slaves in order to free them. After years of religious doubts, he became a Presbyterian after retirement and lived quietly at Wheatland, his brick mansion. He died of pneumonia at age seventy-seven.

Abraham Lincoln

BORN IN LARUE COUNTY, KENTUCKY, 1809
DIED IN WASHINGTON, D.C., 1865

*Best-known lawyer in Illinois;
president during the Civil War; and issuer of the
Emancipation Proclamation, which abolished slavery*

OUR TALLEST PRESIDENT (at six feet four inches) poked fun at his own looks—and the opinion was unanimous.

Skinny and homely, Abraham Lincoln had a wart on his cheek, a scar over one eye (from a fight with a gang of thieves), and a beard that he grew at the suggestion of an eleven-year-old girl. Enemies called him apelike, a "well-meaning baboon." His careless dress didn't help: pants that were often too short, in winter a blue cape or gray shawl fastened with a large safety pin, in summer a linen coat once white.

Very private and undemonstrative, Lincoln was still genuinely interested in people and their problems. He would sit rubbing his chin—a good listener, compassionate, and tolerant. He would also often sit alone, staring out the window for hours. Melancholy moods gave him insomnia and many nightmares.

Lincoln estimated that he had one year altogether of formal education, but he was always passionate about learning. His idea of a best friend was someone who gave you a book you hadn't read yet. In a famous episode, he once walked six miles into the woods to borrow what he had heard was a great grammar book. A few years into his administration, a new kind of book began appearing—collections of Lincoln's witticisms, retold by people who had heard him speak.

The funny books were a result of Lincoln's unique way of breaking up his bouts with depression: storytelling. Always the center of attention in a group, he had jokes, tall tales, and anecdotes for every occasion. When no women were present, his jokes were sometimes about bathrooms or bodily functions, and he loved puns, especially corny ones. Passing a store named for its owner, T. R. Strong, he couldn't resist murmuring, "Coffee are stronger." He really loved to laugh. It filled a need—"I laugh because I must not cry," he once told a friend. His jokes also got him out of answering difficult questions, lightened up tense conversations, and deflected criticism. "That reminds me of a story—," he would say, and be off. His face would light up, his eyes would sparkle, he'd give his hearty high-pitched laugh and sometimes rock back and forth, wrapping his arms around his knees. "He could make a cat laugh!" insisted a witness.

His storytelling skills didn't translate into effective public speaking; his high voice distracted from his words (though the words were always eloquent—notably the 272 of them that make up the Gettysburg Address). Nor was organization a strength; he frequently stashed documents in his stovepipe hat for lack of a proper place. In his office was a pile of papers labeled WHEN YOU CAN'T FIND IT ANYWHERE ELSE, LOOK IN THIS.

Never joining any church, Lincoln read the Bible daily and thought of religion as a totally private matter. He wrestled all his life with questions about race, at first making statements that were clearly racist, later changing his opinions. Once, while on a steamboat ride, he saw ten slaves shackled together and was profoundly affected. He decided the system of slavery was evil: "Whenever I hear anyone arguing for slavery, I feel a strong impulse to see it tried on him personally." He despised war but came to see the Civil War as the only means of keeping the country together.

Hatred of slavery was something he found in Mary Todd. He met her at a party and told her he wanted "in the worst way" to dance with her. They shared much

else—a love of politics and good writing, ambitious goals—but were not always compatible. She cared more than he did about what people thought and was embarrassed when people found Lincoln in his favorite position: stretched out on the floor with a piece of corn bread and a book. He was moody and liked to sit quietly before the fire at night; she was sociable and starved for talk.

Lincoln's inattentiveness drove Mary crazy, and once she even struck him on the nose with a piece of firewood to get him to look at her. Lincoln, ever tolerant, didn't take her temper seriously, but White House staff referred to her as "Her Satanic Majesty" and "the Hellcat." Well educated and a driving force behind the Emancipation Proclamation, which made slavery illegal, Mary was viciously criticized by the press no matter what she did. She was a target of abuse about her looks, taste, and spending habits; her good works were ignored.

Mary and Lincoln had separate beds, in the fashion of well-to-do couples at the time. He used his bedroom as an office, banishing to a guest room the extravagant rosewood bed she'd had made for him. But they remained devoted to each other, and each tried to protect the other from distressing news. She called him "Mr. Lincoln," and he addressed her as "Puss," "Little Woman," and—after the children were born—"Mother."

His own father had been harsh, but Lincoln was frequently heard to say, "It is my pleasure that my children are free, happy, and unrestricted by parental tyranny." He was an indulgent father to his three sons, Robert, Willie, and Tad. Tad came to be known as the "Tyrant of the White House" for his way of twisting his father around his little finger and having fun at others' expense. Lincoln sometimes helped out with child care, which was so unusual for the times that neighbors labeled him "henpecked." He read to the boys, one on each knee, the third on the back of the chair. Or he hauled them up and down the street in a little wagon while he read a book, not always noticing if one of them fell out.

The Lincolns allowed their sons to have all the pets they wanted, including ponies; two pet goats, Nanko and Nanny, who had free run and sometimes barged in on White House receptions; a gray-and-white cat named Bob; and a pet turkey, Jack, that the boys had saved from becoming Thanksgiving dinner.

Lincoln's daily routine began with a small breakfast (coffee and one egg). From early morning to dusk he received long lines of visitors with requests, complaints, news—his palms would become swollen and blistered from shaking so many hands. He sometimes forgot to eat lunch, or made it brief, an apple or a biscuit with a glass of milk. A teetotaler, he most often drank water. Sometimes he went for an afternoon horseback ride or a carriage ride with Mary. After dinner—he ate whatever was put in front of him, though he was partial to oysters and fricasseed chicken—he usually went back to his office for several more hours. Sometimes he wrapped his gray shawl around his shoulders and walked over to the War Department, without escort or guard, to follow the progress of the increasingly bloody Civil War. Getting back to Mary by midnight, he'd discuss the day with her. Besides swapping jokes, Lincoln relaxed by playing chess and rarely missed an opportunity to see a play, slipping into theaters unannounced and sitting in a specially provided rocking chair.

After Willie became the only child ever to die in the White House (from typhoid), his parents were distraught. Mary became increasingly unstable and met often with spiritualists, trying to reach her son's spirit. Lincoln, deeply interested in psychic phenomena, attended several séances with her. The war took its toll on the White House, which gradually went shabby, with bugs in the furniture and tobacco juice stains around the spittoons.

Five days after the war ended, Lincoln went to Ford's Theatre in Washington to see Our American Cousin, a popular comedy of the day. He sat in his rocking chair, holding hands with Mary. As usual, one line got the biggest laugh: "Well, I guess I know enough to turn you inside out, old gal—you sockdologizing old man trap," said one character. The laughter covered the sound of a shot fired into Lincoln's head by John Wilkes Booth, a mentally unbalanced actor who detested Lincoln's views against slavery, as many people did at the time. Lincoln died nine hours later, at age fifty-six, without regaining consciousness—the first president to die by assassination.

Because he is now regarded as one of our greatest presidents, it is hard to imagine how disliked Lincoln was during his lifetime. He received death threats even before he was elected and got more than ten thousand of them afterward. Considering the threats a novelty, he kept some of them in his desk in an envelope labeled "Assassinations," but he also directed secretaries to toss out threatening letters without showing them to him. He believed that a president should not be shielded from people and took few safety precautions. "I cannot bring myself to believe that any human being lives who would do me any harm," he said.

Andrew Johnson

BORN IN RALEIGH, NORTH CAROLINA, 1808
DIED IN CARTER'S STATION, TENNESSEE, 1875

ALTHOUGH ANDREW JOHNSON never attended a day of school in his life, he did know how to sew better than any other president. He was sold by his impoverished parents and apprenticed to a tailor at age fourteen. He later ran away and grew up to open his own tailor shop. Eliza (the First Lady who married at the youngest age—sixteen) taught him how to read and write in the early days of their marriage; he would sew during his lessons. Johnson became the only president who knew how to quilt and who made his own suits (a skill he was fiercely proud of—he dressed neatly, usually in black).

He appeared cold—White House staff labeled him "the Grim Presence"—but loaned money to those in need and identified with underdogs. Instead of evicting mice he found inside, he would leave flour and water out for them. He belonged to no particular church but attended various services. He was fond of the circus, playing checkers, and growing his own vegetables.

Eliza, stricken with tuberculosis, kept herself nearly invisible. Martha, one of the five Johnson children, acted as hostess and oversaw the White House cows. Eliza made rare appearances at the breakfast table, but mostly stayed upstairs, sewing, reading, and clipping newspapers and magazine articles. Twice a day, Johnson stopped in to go over current events with her; at night she showed him articles favorable to him, saving the (increasingly) negative ones for the morning so he wouldn't lose sleep.

In the turbulent years after the Civil War, Johnson became so unpopular that he was the only president to be impeached by the Senate (but not convicted or removed from office). There were no apparent hard feelings, for he was the only ex-president to later serve as a senator. He died of a stroke at age sixty-six.

Ulysses S. Grant

BORN IN POINT PLEASANT, OHIO, 1822
DIED NEAR SARATOGA, NEW YORK, 1885

*Professional soldier and popular
Civil War hero who became president; considered the
creator of modern American warfare*

ALTHOUGH HE SAW MANY battles as a famous military man, gentle Ulysses Grant couldn't stand the sight of animal blood. He didn't even like to eat meat that wasn't well-done. (Eating two-legged animals was completely out of the question—which ruled out fowl.) As a child he did every chore related to horses, his forte, and avoided at all costs his father's tannery, where bloody hides made him ill. He did not take to hunting, which made him feel like a "failure" in a society that valued hunters.

Grant grew up to fail at many jobs he tried. One Christmas he was so poor he had to pawn his gold watch for twenty-two dollars so he could give his family presents. A graduate of the U.S. Military Academy at West Point, he volunteered for the Civil War and was at first rejected—possibly because of his reputation as a heavy drinker. Eventually acclaimed as the man most responsible for winning the Civil War, he became thought of as someone who could do no wrong. There was much gossip about his drinking on the battlefield, but President Lincoln always defended General U. S. "Unconditional Surrender" Grant against those who wanted him out: "I need this man. He fights."

Grant became the first president to have a woman run against him during a campaign (Victoria Woodhull) and later the first president whose term was marked by major scandal. Though he wasn't personally responsible, his is believed to be the most corrupt administration up to that time. Grant felt compelled to issue a written defense, arguing that any mistakes "have been errors of judgment, not of intent."

Full of contradictions, he had his own sense of honor; when his father parceled out his estate, Grant declined his share on the grounds that he hadn't earned the money. A professional soldier, he seldom swore, didn't like dirty jokes, and always bathed alone in his tent, making a point of not letting others see him. Tone-deaf, he had trouble marching to military music. He rarely went to church but became a Methodist late in life. He did not support slavery (he freed a slave given him by his father-in-law) but did not believe in racial equality. Superstitious, he thought it was bad luck to retrace one's steps.

In public Grant was a man of notoriously few words. A whole speech once was: "Gentlemen, in response, it will be impossible to do more than thank you." Another time he stood and announced, "I rise only to say I do not intend to say anything." He didn't like being alone, in formal settings, or around people with more education than he had. He preferred the company of family and close friends.

The person with the most influence on him was his wife, Julia Dent. He rarely allowed her to interfere in politics but took her advice on all else. They did almost everything together, teased and flirted in public, and had a large assortment of pet names for each other. When she wanted to have surgery to correct the uncontrollable movement of her eye, he insisted he loved her as she was. She could get him to talk more by deliberately telling a story wrong—he would jump in and retell it, and she would sit back, satisfied. When they weren't together and she needed to ask him something, she would stick a note into an envelope, mark it "The President, Immediate," and have a staff member deliver it.

Grant affectionately pampered his four children, usually giving them whatever they wanted. "I am almost crazy sometimes to see Fred," he wrote during an absence from a son; the two oldest sons were away at college during the White House years. The younger children, Nellie (treated like a little princess, with midnight dancing parties) and Jesse (a prankster who talked back to his father), were high-spirited. In the evening the family would lounge in Julia's bedroom for teasing, storytelling, and gossiping—their favorite time of day. Grant and Jesse also liked to spend hours on the roof, observing the stars through a powerful telescope, until Julia would send a messenger up to fetch them both to bed. Jesse's pets were often as rambunctious as he was. Many of his dogs died mysteriously until Grant informed the White House staff that everyone would be fired if any more died—then the dogs began to live to old age.

Julia tried to make the White House brighter and cheerier with more pillows and newfangled additions like closets. She and Grant liked a showy, unrestrained style of entertaining and gave dinner parties featuring as many as twenty-nine courses. At the extravagant wedding for Nellie, they served soft-shell crab, four kinds of meat, and a magnificent cake served with chocolate pudding. The White House stables held Grant's favorite horses—Butcher Boy, Cincinnatus (a gift from Cincinnati citizens), Egypt, St. Louis, and others.

On their last day in the White House—when they lingered so long some thought they would never leave—Grant and Julia admitted to each other that they felt like waifs. To cheer up, they launched themselves on a round-the-world tour, deliberately unplanned, during which Grant was hailed everywhere as the world's greatest living military figure.

Once retired, Grant lived simply. Cucumbers soaked in vinegar were a favorite breakfast. He liked to draw and paint and go riding (often speeding, he once had to pay a twenty-dollar fine). Julia must not have minded cigar smoke, as he smoked twenty cigars a day.

While eating a peach one morning, he noticed a pain in his throat. During his slow death from mouth cancer, Grant raced to write his memoirs, hoping to give Julia some financial security. With typical determination, he finished the book three days before he died, at age sixty-three. Where was Grant buried? In Grant's Tomb, on Riverside Drive, a major New York City tourist attraction for many years afterward. His memoirs were a huge best-seller, and the profits took care of Julia for the rest of her life.

Rutherford B. Hayes

BORN IN DELAWARE, OHIO, 1822; DIED IN FREMONT, OHIO, 1893

WITH WHISKERS SO LONG they dipped into his soup, Hayes was the first president to use the telephone. His phone number was "1." Lucy, the first college-educated First Lady, supported the women's rights movement, except for the right to vote— Hayes disapproved. They banned alcohol, smoking, dancing, and cards at their austere White House, but did preside (with their five children) over the first Easter-egg roll on the lawn.

James A. Garfield

BORN IN CUYAHOGA COUNTY, OHIO, 1831; DIED IN ELBERON, NEW JERSEY, 1881

GARFIELD WOULD GREET people by barking, just like his dog, Veto. The first president to campaign in English and Spanish and to be left-handed, he loved to hug. He appreciated his wife, Lucretia's, intellect but had old-fashioned ideas about women. Both preferred evenings with their five children, reading and playing cards. He was assassinated at age forty-nine, dying of blood poisoning from his gunshot wound.

Chester A. Arthur

BORN IN FAIRFIELD, VERMONT, 1830; DIED IN NEW YORK CITY, 1886

ARTHUR'S FONDNESS FOR late-night feasts of mutton chops was exceeded only by his love for long talks. His wife, Ellen, died suddenly two years before he became president. He tried to make the White House cheery but cried easily. Nicknamed "Elegant Arthur," he had eighty pairs of pants and changed clothes often. Many judged him the best fisherman in America. He retired to "raise big pumpkins" but died a year later.

Grover Cleveland

BORN IN CALDWELL, NEW JERSEY, 1837; DIED IN PRINCETON, NEW JERSEY, 1908

THE ONLY PRESIDENT TO serve two nonconsecutive terms, Cleveland was also the only one to marry in the White House. Frances (Frank), twenty-seven years younger, brightened the dreary atmosphere, raised their five children (he supported another who may have been his illegitimate son), and tried to keep him from wearing his orange suit. Overweight, blunt, and quick-tempered, he suffered many ailments.

Benjamin Harrison

BORN IN NORTH BEND, OHIO, 1833; DIED IN INDIANAPOLIS, INDIANA, 1901

THE "HUMAN ICEBERG," Harrison never forgot that much was expected of him as the grandson of a president. Stiff in public, he indulged his grandchildren and his artist wife in private. Caroline painted china and filled White House parties with orchids. The Harrisons installed electric lights but were too afraid of shocks to ever turn them off. After Caroline died, Harrison shocked everyone by marrying her niece.

William McKinley

BORN IN NILES, OHIO, 1843; DIED IN BUFFALO, NEW YORK, 1901

MCKINLEY'S DEVOTION TO his wife, Ida, was so saintly that other husbands complained that he made them look bad. During her epileptic seizures, her husband would protect her from potential embarrassment by calmly draping his handkerchief over her head. Their White House was sober; the color yellow was banned. Ida managed to outlive two daughters as well as McKinley—he was assassinated at age fifty-eight.

Theodore Roosevelt

BORN IN NEW YORK CITY, 1858
DIED IN OYSTER BAY, NEW YORK, 1919

Rancher, hunter, adventurer,
national hero after the Spanish-American War,
vice president, and activist president

THEODORE ("TEDDY") ROOSEVELT lived life with such gusto that some assumed he must be faking his enthusiasm. Others wondered if he was insane or had a drinking problem. (He didn't, and once sued a magazine for calling him drunk.) He loved the limelight and was reported to relish being "the bride at every wedding, the corpse at every funeral." His clothes, manners, and accent all gave the impression of a bookish, priggish wimp who stayed indoors—and he did love to read. He finished two or three books a day and knew the Bible well, as a member of the Dutch Reformed Church. But as the youngest president up to that time, as well as the most adventurous and zesty, he also had boundless energy and no fear.

Making up for his asthmatic childhood, Roosevelt advocated a strenuous lifestyle. He boxed regularly until a hard blow blinded his left eye, then took up jujitsu, tennis, and rowing. He engaged his guests in "scrambles"—races over rough terrain, the rule being that you had to climb, swim, or jump every obstacle. His energetic dancing style was described by one partner as "hopping." He once went ahead with an hour-long speech after being shot in the chest—finishing the speech before going to a hospital. He carried a revolver, hoping to shoot before getting shot. He was the first president to go up in an airplane and down in a submarine, the first to visit a foreign country while in office, and the first to ride in a car.

He married Alice Lee, who died three years later during childbirth; distraught, Roosevelt never mentioned her again, even to their daughter, Alice. He had five children with his second wife, Edith Carow, who was calm and dignified while he was impulsive and extravagant; people said she was "born mature," and he remained "about seven years old." She sorted his mail, read to him from the papers, and influenced him greatly, careful never to call attention to her role.

Roosevelt had breakfast—a soup-size bowl of peaches and cream—with his family, then took a short walk and went to work. He made a point of laughing "a hundred times a day"—or even roaring, doubled over, his face red. In the afternoon he held meetings while he was shaved, the barber taking care to back off when Roosevelt gestured too vigorously.

Fatherhood was yet another grand adventure, and he permitted the most rambunctious White House ever—so wild that some wondered if the building could withstand the strain. At four o'clock he would stop whatever he was doing and devote the "children's hour" to his six "blessed bunnies." He would start out reading from his favorite book (*The Wind in the Willows*) or telling stories about his youthful escapades in the Wild West, and end with hair-raising ghost stories, pillow fights, and wrestling. "I play bear with the children almost every night," he admitted. Games of hide-and-seek (he always wanted to be "it") were held in the attic, and when the children were in bed with the measles, he kept them entertained by reenacting Civil War battles with miniature ships and war toys.

At dinner he savored talk that was fresh and uninhibited, surrounded by a mix of people: boxers, writers, scientists, cowboys, university presidents, lumbermen. Sometimes they dined on bear meat or turtles, sometimes on simpler fare—clear soup, grilled fish, Irish stew, pork and beans. He was known to drink four glasses of milk at one sitting.

Roosevelt so loved animals that he once planned to be a zoologist, inspired the name for small stuffed (teddy) bears, and presided over the White House's largest and most eclectic menagerie of creatures both exotic and ordinary. The first thing he did upon retirement, however, was to go on safari with his son Kermit to East Africa, where they shot more than five hundred animals.

Years later, at his estate at Sagamore Hill, weakened by multiple ailments—and by grief over the death of Quentin, his youngest son, during World War I—Roosevelt died of a stroke at age sixty. His last words were "Please put out the light."

William H. Taft

BORN IN CINCINNATI, OHIO, 1857
DIED IN WASHINGTON, D.C., 1930

OUR LARGEST PRESIDENT (332 pounds at his peak), William Taft was nonetheless athletic. He learned to surf in Waikiki, danced and played tennis well, and was both the first president to take up golf and the first to throw the ceremonial ball that opens baseball season. Cleaning up after playing sports could be a problem—he once got stuck in the bathtub and had White House plumbers install a replacement that could hold four average-size people. Fresh milk (from Mooly Wooly, the last of the White House cows) and huge steaks for breakfast gave him energy—but not always enough to keep him awake. Nicknamed "Sleeping Beauty," he fell asleep at funerals, once slept right through a typhoon, and eventually even died in his sleep. He was frequently depressed and irritable in the White House, because he didn't really want to be there. In public he called it "the lonesomest place in the world." In private he admitted, "Politics makes me sick."

Helen ("Nellie") was his opposite—small and ambitious. She attended all his meetings (with the excuse that someone had to nudge him awake), terrorized the White House staff (demanding that everything be spotless and dignified), poured energy into their three children, and delighted Washington neighbors with their first cherry-blossom display, planting two trees herself. After she had a stroke and needed a year to recover, Taft spent part of each day telling her funny stories, helping her learn to talk again.

Upon retirement, he lost ninety pounds, regained his cheerful ways and infectious chuckle, and became chief justice of the Supreme Court—the job he had wanted all along.

Woodrow Wilson

BORN IN STAUNTON, VIRGINIA, 1856
DIED IN WASHINGTON, D.C., 1924

*Professor, president of Princeton University,
governor of New Jersey, and leader of the United States
during World War I*

WOODROW WILSON WAS nine before the alphabet started making sense to him. Possibly dyslexic, he grew up to become a political science scholar, the most popular member of his college's faculty, and our most highly educated president—his family budget always showed greater expenses for books than for clothes.

A devout Presbyterian, he prayed on his knees every morning and night and believed that God had foreordained him president—a forceful, commanding presence to lead the United States through stormy times. Sometimes cold and dour in public, preferring talk of familiar things amid the company of family and old friends, he shied away from meeting new people. Believing that women should be subservient to men, he firmly opposed the right of women to vote (but later found it politically useful to mellow his stance and was president when women did start voting). Breaking his promises to black voters for reform, he used his power to make government more segregated, not less. He met with African American leaders only once, and it ended in bitterness.

Wilson often felt both grateful and guilty that his first wife, Ellen Axson, gave up a promising career as a painter to marry him. She managed their home so well that his only chore was to wind the tall clock each week. After a morning of proofreading his writing together, they would talk with punctuation marks at lunch: "The soup comma my dear comma is excellent period." In the White House, they maintained separate bedrooms. Wilson's three daughters worshiped him, and in the evenings they all played pool, clowned around in games of charades, sang, and read aloud. Wilson would sit on the floor in front of the fire, rocking back and forth while he recited poetry.

When Ellen died at age fifty-four of kidney disease, Wilson sobbed uncontrollably at her funeral. He confided to an aide that he hoped to be assassinated, because he didn't think he could go on. But a little more than a year later (causing a flood of gossip and rumors), he proposed to Edith Galt, a jewelry-store owner who had two years of formal schooling and was the first woman in Washington to drive her own car. Considering thirteen his lucky number, Wilson had her select a diamond engagement ring from thirteen choices. He soon regained his poise and was seen dancing on and off curbs and heard whistling vaudeville tunes.

He treated Edith as a coworker; she was at his side on every public occasion and worked closely with him in private. He listened carefully when she talked, and when they walked he took small, fast steps to match hers. They slept in Lincoln's bed, which they moved into Wilson's room. Setting an example for government rationing during World War I, they endured gasless Sundays, meatless Mondays, and wheatless Tuesdays. To save the energy of mowing, they kept a herd of sheep (including tobacco-chewing Old Ike) munching the lawn; Wilson would sometimes wander out to pat their woolly heads.

Never robust, but with a forcefully positive attitude about his poor health, Wilson suffered a major stroke while president. Ironically (because she also vigorously opposed the right of women to vote), Edith took over significant presidential duties. In a controversial cover-up of Wilson's true condition (for at least a month he was totally disabled, watching movies in his sickroom, preferring old films of himself during tours abroad), she screened all visitors and decided what (if anything) was important enough to inform him about. Was she our first woman president and was he the "First Man"? How much business did she really do? Indignant when these questions were raised, Edith nevertheless refused to allow Wilson to resign.

After two more years, they retired to a brick-and-limestone home in Washington. There Edith nursed Wilson until his death three years later at age sixty-seven. "The machinery is worn out—I am ready" were his last coherent words.

Warren G. Harding

BORN IN CORSICA, OHIO, 1865; DIED IN SAN FRANCISCO, CALIFORNIA, 1923

USUALLY REGARDED AS our worst president, Harding soaked up scandal. He joined the Ku Klux Klan, gambled away White House china, and spent days golfing instead of working. He was unhappily married to Florence ("Flossie"), who consulted astrologers, put him down in public, and tended bar at his poker parties. Rumors that she poisoned him or that he committed suicide were false, but gossip about his many affairs was true.

Calvin Coolidge

BORN IN PLYMOUTH, VERMONT, 1872; DIED IN NORTHAMPTON, MASSACHUSETTS, 1933

"HOW CAN THEY TELL?" asked a writer who heard that Coolidge had died. Famously silent, he was sarcastically dubbed "Smiley" by White House staff. Grace, a teacher of deaf children, had no role in his work, and he was a strict father to their two sons. Despite his subdued nature, he liked to walk around with a raccoon around his neck—and he rode a mechanical horse almost every day, whooping like a cowboy.

Herbert Hoover

BORN IN WEST BRANCH, IOWA, 1874; DIED IN NEW YORK CITY, 1964

THE PRESIDENT ONCE introduced as "Hoobert Heever" was reserved, formal, and a millionaire from his mining expertise. He and his wife, Lou, a fellow geologist, often dined with so many guests that cooks would resort to "White House Supreme Surprise" (leftovers). He had a soft heart but hated showing it in public. Upon his death, he left Shangri-la, his summer place in the Blue Ridge Mountains, to the government.

Franklin D. Roosevelt

BORN IN HYDE PARK, NEW YORK, 1882
DIED IN WARM SPRINGS, GEORGIA, 1945

*Leader during twelve of the most difficult
years in American history, when crises included
the Great Depression and World War II*

PRESIDENT LONGER THAN anyone else, Franklin Roosevelt was his era's biggest hero, with grand gestures and a jaunty, fearless grin. Inspired by his dashing cousin, he copied some of Theodore's habits, followed the same career path, and even married Theodore's niece, Eleanor. Radiating confidence and energy, he delighted in his job. "Wouldn't you be president if you could?" he once asked a friend. "Wouldn't anybody?"

Roosevelt was so dynamic that people would forget he couldn't stand up or walk without help. At age thirty-nine he had been struck with polio, leaving his legs permanently crippled and making him our only disabled president. He developed a remarkable way of distracting attention from his wheelchair, and few photos exist of him in it—yet his disability had a major impact on his life. He had to have his pajamas put on for him; to travel he had to be lifted in and out of cars; he was unable to get to restaurants for the rich food he loved (quail, pheasant, oyster crabs, hard-to-find cheeses); even standing was a challenging ordeal. Much more afraid of fire than of assassination, he would spend hours practicing crawling out of a room in case he had to face a fire alone.

Via the latest technology—radio—Roosevelt's rich voice made him an intimate guest in living rooms everywhere. During his "fireside chats," Americans stopped whatever they were doing to listen to the broadcasts, which were of great comfort during the grim days of the Great Depression and the terrifying events of World War II.

His White House style was relaxed and informal, and he loved to joke, gossip, and play. He wore favorite old sweaters even after they got holey, and he kept a collection of miniature pigs in his bedroom. He had several hobbies but was an especially avid stamp collector—amassing more than twenty-five thousand in forty albums. Between his daily swim in the White House pool and dinnertime, he liked a martini; he smoked more than a pack of cigarettes a day. An Episcopalian, he loved singing hymns ("Faith of Our Fathers" was a favorite) and resented being ogled in church: "I can do almost everything in the goldfish bowl of the president's life," he said, "but I'll be hanged if I can say my prayers in it."

On evenings alone he worked on his stamp albums or assembled models of sailing ships. When he was sleepless, which happened often during the most destructive war in history, a ritual helped him fall asleep: He would imagine himself as a boy at Hyde Park, the Roosevelt family estate, physically conquering his fears by sledding down a steep hill over and over. His Scottish terrier, Fala, slept in his room at night. (His German shepherd, Major, had been exiled after biting one too many guests—and ripping the pants of the British prime minister.)

Roosevelt called Eleanor "Babs" (short for "Baby") and rated her "the most extraordinarily interesting woman" he knew. But she and Roosevelt were very different and led independent lives, with separate bedrooms. Shy and serious, with primary responsibility for raising their six children, she did not have a playful relationship with him. When she learned of his affair with her secretary, she took on more of an activist role rather than divorce him (which would have ruined his career), and became the first First Lady to have a public life of her own.

She began writing and lecturing (donating her earnings—which usually topped the president's—to charity), and most of all pressuring her husband to take action on social reforms she was passionate about. Women, blacks, poor people, and young people all came to think of her as a special friend. She traveled so much that a newspaper once jokingly printed the headline "Mrs. Roosevelt Spends Night at the White House!" She often communicated with the president by way of an "Eleanor basket" next to his bed, where she put memos and reports she wanted him to read. He teased her and sometimes wished she weren't "so darn busy" so he could see her more, but he rarely tried to curb her activities and never allowed anyone to criticize her in his presence. Roosevelt, according to one sharp-tongued relative, was "two-thirds mush and one-third Eleanor," and their marriage was more partnership than romance. Their children grew up to have a total of nineteen marriages among them.

Roosevelt liked to surround himself with admiring, amiable women—among whom the housekeeper at the White House did not seem to be one. Over and over, she had the cooks serve plain and overcooked food he disliked. He got oatmeal every breakfast, until he finally sent her coupons and a memo listing other cereals. She kept serving broccoli after he said he hated it because she thought "he *should* like it." He couldn't bring himself to fire her, but would sometimes disappear after meals to rustle up egg sandwiches somewhere else.

In failing health, as the war finally drew to a close, Roosevelt began sleeping ten hours a night and limiting his workday to four hours. He spent more time at Warm Springs, his second home and a rehabilitation center for polio victims. One afternoon, when he was sixty-three, after a lunch of gruel and cream, he suffered a stroke while going over some papers. In the presence of three women (an artist sketching his portrait, a cousin crocheting nearby, and Eleanor's former secretary), he said, "I have a terrific pain in the back of my head." He died within hours. He had been president so long that people—especially children, who had known no other leader—were staggered.

He left most of his $2 million estate to Eleanor. She lived on as the most admired and influential woman of her time—one of the first American delegates to the United Nations, the world's foremost spokesperson for human rights, and companion to twenty-three grandchildren and great-grandchildren.

Harry S. Truman

BORN IN LAMAR, MISSOURI, 1884
DIED IN KANSAS CITY, MISSOURI, 1972

*Senator, then vice president
who became president during the final months
of World War II, after Roosevelt's death*

HARRY TRUMAN SPENT HIS childhood playing piano. Because of the thick, expensive glasses he wore from age six on, he wasn't allowed to play contact sports and endured much teasing. He escaped into "tickling the ivories," as he said, and thought about becoming a concert pianist. But even though he was musically talented and well read (he had read every book in his local library by age fifteen), his first forty years consisted of failed attempts at farming and business. Politics gave him a stable job, and the White House was the first (though temporary) home of his own.

A little surprised when others took him seriously, Truman had a knack for making hard choices. Whether to drop two atomic bombs on Japan was one of the toughest decisions a president has ever faced, but Truman said he never lost sleep over it and believed that it ended World War II. For a short time he had on his desk a sign that said THE BUCK STOPS HERE—and showed that he took the idea seriously by assuming responsibility for numerous postwar changes. He struggled to overcome racial and ethnic stereotypes he had held early in his career and ultimately made courageous civil rights decisions. Earnest, folksy, and more popular than he or anyone else thought, he won an unexpected second term in the greatest election upset in American history.

A Baptist, he met his future wife, Bess Wallace, in Sunday school when they were five and six. They put off marriage for another thirty years. Talkative and witty in private (she laughed so hard her whole body would shake), she seemed ill at ease and grim when in the public eye. No-nonsense Bess believed that "a woman's place in public is to sit beside her husband, be silent, and be sure her hat is on straight." Truman, however, called her "the Boss," seldom made a decision without consulting her, and esteemed her as a "full partner . . . politically and otherwise." She shopped alone and unnoticed in Washington department stores, loved to read mysteries, went to every baseball game she could fit into her schedule, and liked to listen to Truman play the piano. (He brought three pianos to the White House and was probably the best pianist of all the presidents.) He treasured nights with her after his days of "doing at least one hundred things I didn't want to do." They shared the same White House bedroom, and their closets were notoriously messy.

They expected perfect table manners of their only child, Margaret—except when watermelon was served for dessert and the family would have seed wars. White House staff called them "the Three Musketeers" because they spent so much time together. Margaret got nearly everything she wanted, except the one Christmas when Truman bought her a baby grand piano (she had requested an electric train). She became a singer and author of murder mysteries (including *Murder in the White House*). Her father supported her singing ambitions, and when a music critic roasted her in print, he fired off a letter warning that the man would need "a new nose" if Truman ever met him. Truman got his peppery nickname—"Give-'Em-Hell Harry"—for the way he treated opponents and those outside his home, not those in it; the family atmosphere was calm and close-knit. His staff members called him "a decent human being." He enjoyed chatting with the Secret Service agents who accompanied him on his walk every morning—two miles at a clip of 128 steps a minute.

Smug about his trim waistline, Truman watched what he ate. He did like a glass of bourbon in the mornings (possibly believing that bourbon was good for circulation) and sometimes indulged in hot southern biscuits (which replaced the traditional cold, hard White House dinner rolls), peach cobbler, angel food cake (his favorite dessert), and Bess's "Ozark Pudding," made with apples. He had dozens of suits—his one indulgence—tailor-made to show off how fit he was. Always described as dapper and crisp, he wore a hat and walked with a bounce. After falling in love with Key West, Florida, he favored loud shirts with colorful tropical patterns.

Despite his positive nature, Truman did get irritated by certain things: jazz, modern art (which he disparaged as "ham and eggs art"), some artists ("half-baked lazy people"), women who smoked or drank (his approval when Bess wanted to bob her hair was reluctant), dentists, brussels sprouts, guns, snobs, his looks (he thought he had a "girl mouth"), the telephone (he loathed the sound of the ring), the typewriter (he gave up trying to use it), and the "Missouri Waltz" (which was always played in his honor but annoyed him so much it made him twitch). As musical as he was, he reportedly was not a good singer and never learned to dance.

Truman's favorite game by far was poker. But even better was to have lots of good books around, a comfortable chair, and a good light. Margaret could not recall her father at home without a book in his hand. Although he had no formal education beyond high school, he knew American history and geography inside out and, on a plane, could look out at any time and name the region he was flying over. Sometimes he wished he had been a history teacher (instead of a history maker).

The longer he was president, the more time-conscious he got; he had nine clocks in his office by the end of his second term. Honest almost to a fault, he could be petty and unpredictable, and he gradually grew unpopular. After retirement, he and Bess were steady patrons of the Independence (Missouri) Public Library. Neighbors out for evening walks could see him in the window, sitting with a book under a reading lamp.

He died at age eighty-eight of multiple ailments. His estate of $600,000 was divided between Bess and Margaret.

Dwight D. Eisenhower

BORN IN DENISON, TEXAS, 1890
DIED IN WASHINGTON, D.C., 1969

*The Supreme Commander of the Allied forces
and greatest American military hero of World War II;
the natural choice for next president*

AS A PROFESSIONAL SOLDIER, Dwight Eisenhower was used to being taken care of. He didn't drive, didn't know how to use a phone, didn't handle money, and didn't dress himself. Supermarkets and Laundromats were foreign territory. At West Point (where his main interest was football, not a military career), he was not a model cadet; he received many demerits for smoking (he smoked four packs a day until he quit thirty years later), tardiness, and whirling dance partners too vigorously around the ballroom.

"I hate war," he once said, "as only a soldier who has lived it can, only as one who has seen its brutality, its futility, its *stupidity*." Feeling the emotion and loss of war so deeply, he decided a commander should motivate his troops by radiating self-confidence and cheer. Tending to credit others for his mounting successes, he referred to himself as "a simple country boy," "a dumb bunny," and "an old dodo." He seldom spoke ill of anyone—the only man he ever truly hated was Nazi leader Adolf Hitler—and was distressed when anyone didn't like him. Most people found it impossible not to like "Ike."

Less than a month after he wed Mary Doud, known as Mamie, Eisenhower told her that his country would always come first; she came second. During the first thirty-five years of their marriage the Eisenhowers moved a total of thirty-five times, with an uncomplaining Mamie winning over endless neighbors with informal dinners. He believed that a wife's role was to center her life around her husband, and so did she: "I have only one career," Mamie often said, "and his name is Ike." He never discussed his professional life with her and seldom even saw her in daylight, but he counted on her loyal support. She tried to make his time off quietly cozy, and he seldom brought work home. He enjoyed pampering her, except when it came to playing bridge (he tended to yell at her mistakes) and her valuable collection of porcelain birds (he thought they were dust collectors). They slept in a custom-made double bed—Mamie said she liked to reach out at night "and pat Ike on his old bald head anytime I want to."

Eisenhower wrote Mamie 319 letters during the three war years they were apart. But every time she saw his picture in the newspaper, he was with his female driver, who, amid much gossip, went nearly everywhere with him. After the war he never saw the driver again, and Eisenhower never confirmed or denied a relationship. On his fortieth wedding anniversary he had the words "I love you better today than the day I met you" engraved on a ruby heart for his wife.

Eisenhower rose at six o'clock every morning, careful not to awaken Mamie. Possibly believing that rest would prevent wrinkles, she spent a good part of her day in bed, wearing a pink robe—her trademark color—and a matching ribbon in her hair. Her nickname among White House staff was "Sleeping Beauty." She would stop whatever she was doing each day to watch As the World Turns, her favorite soap opera. She couldn't cook, except for fudge, cakes from a mix, and baked potatoes. But one of Eisenhower's hobbies was cooking, and Mamie had a special kitchen installed for him in the White House. He was famous for cornmeal pancakes, amazing vegetable soups, and charbroiled steaks; his favorite dessert was prune whip. He bolted whatever food was put in front of him—unless he had done the cooking, when he took time to savor his creations.

Other hobbies included oil painting—he claimed he hadn't the "faintest semblance of talent," but found it the best way to relax and be alone. He played so much golf that the U.S. Golf Association built a green for him near the White House, and he was so annoyed by squirrels that dug holes there that the staff came up with Operation Squirrel Seduction, then Operation Exodus, to get rid of them. The White House dogs were Heidi, a weimaraner, and Spunky, a Scottie.

Eisenhower mixed easily with all kinds of people, but most liked being with successful, self-confident men. His closest friends were self-made millionaires who took him on frequent hunting and fishing trips to scenic places. Though he was known to end conversations abruptly, he was as sunny as his lopsided smile and hearty laugh hinted. He worked hard to control his anger, and any signs of it were subtle—jabbing a pencil so hard that it broke, or flinching after getting slapped on the back (he hated overfamiliarity). He wore expensive, custom-made clothes given him by manufacturers, and he seldom wore a suit more than twice. A Presbyterian, Eisenhower formally composed his own prayers and called himself "the most intensely religious man I know."

He showered affection on his first son, nicknamed "Icky"; when the boy died of scarlet fever at age three, Eisenhower called it the greatest disaster of his life. He was extremely proud of his second son, John (who became a diplomat and author), and of his four grandchildren. He had a special relationship with grandson David, sharing long, serious talks and a way of shaking hands while they both bowed so low that David sometimes fell over. He liked everything about grown-up David except his long hair and once offered him one hundred dollars if he would cut it (David obliged but his grandfather thought it was still too long so didn't pay up). Eisenhower renamed Shangri-la, the presidential weekend retreat, Camp David, in his grandson's honor.

Upon his retirement, a farm at Gettysburg, Pennsylvania, became the Eisenhowers' final home. He wrote his memoirs and spent hours with Mamie on the sunporch, watching television and painting. While president, he had a moderate heart attack; after retirement he had six more attacks, each one leaving him weaker. He died at age seventy-nine of heart failure. His last words to Mamie were, "I've always loved my wife. I've always loved my children. I've always loved my grandchildren. And I have always loved my country." He left the bulk of his estate—nearly $3 million—to her.

John F. Kennedy

BORN IN BROOKLINE, MASSACHUSETTS, 1917
DIED IN DALLAS, TEXAS, 1963

➤★

*World War II navy commander, senator, and
the youngest elected president, whose term of less than three years
continues to inspire and fascinate*

ALTHOUGH HE PRESENTED an image of athletic vigor and energy in public, John Kennedy often spent more than half the day in bed and sometimes had to use crutches to get about. With a potentially fatal adrenal gland failure, he suffered frequent infections and fevers of up to 106 degrees. One leg was shorter than the other, and his chronic back pain, aggravated by a World War II injury, required him to wear a back brace and to get up to five shots a day deep in his muscles. He found that sitting in a rocking chair eased the pain and had a chair available wherever he went. He used a sunlamp daily to get his healthy glow, and the way he looked—tan, handsome, with thick, glossy hair—helped him win the closest presidential election in American history.

A millionaire by age twenty-one, Kennedy was our wealthiest president. The only president besides George Washington to decline his salary, he donated his to the Boy Scouts and Girl Scouts, the United Negro College Fund, and Jewish organizations. He never paid his own bills and would set off on a trip without a penny, assuming that friends would pay for things (they did, and were later reimbursed by his office in New York). The first Roman Catholic president at a time when Catholicism was believed an insurmountable barrier to the presidency, he rarely spoke of his religious beliefs and attended Protestant services occasionally. A strong supporter of civil rights, he was the first president to speak openly and passionately about the contradiction between the status of African Americans and the ideals of American freedom.

Why did Kennedy occasionally bark like a seal for two minutes straight? Though he was charming and witty, he didn't think he was a good public speaker; to prepare for high office, he hired a drama coach to help him with voice exercises—of which barking was one. At other times he would put on a silk bathrobe, have a brandy, smoke a cigar, and speak along with recordings of famous speeches in history. He took numerous showers a day, and would completely change clothes each time. He wore fashionable, custom-made European suits, and his circle of friends was glamorous—young, rich, and well educated.

Kennedy delayed announcing his engagement to Jacqueline Bouvier as a favor to the *Saturday Evening Post,* which had scheduled an article on his exciting bachelor life. Jackie quit her job writing a daily column of interviews and announced, "My life revolves around my husband." She got him to stop skipping meals, get better haircuts, and improve his manners (he tended to walk several feet ahead, leaving her to open doors herself). She developed what she called the "PBO" (Polite Brush-Off) to avoid situations she didn't like, mostly encounters with "boring" politicians. Americans were obsessed with her style—her whispery voice, trademark sunglasses, shockingly expensive designer clothes from New York and Paris, and pillbox hats. She received so much mail about her hair that she issued a statement: "What does my hairdo have to do with my husband's ability to be president?" Yet she was known to send locks of hair in advance of trips so that hairdressers would be prepared.

She transformed the White House into a center for the arts, with gatherings of artists, writers, and musicians. She brought chefs who knew French cooking into the kitchen, although, due to stomach trouble, Kennedy stuck to a bland diet (Jackie called it "children's food")—he loved soups, especially fish chowder. His attention span was short, and although after dinner they often had private movie screenings, he usually left in the middle, saying, "All right, let's haul it out of here." He was a famously speedy reader and preferred meetings to be brief and held in hallways.

The Kennedys lived independent lives and had separate bedrooms. His was decorated in dark blue and white, and the music from the stereo speakers under the bed ranged from Peggy Lee or Frank Sinatra to country-and-western songs, show tunes, and German military music. Kennedy didn't like to be alone; his frequent extramarital affairs weren't made public for many years.

Jackie's room was pale blue and green and had a bench at the foot of the bed for her stacks of art and fashion magazines. She took foreign vacations and spent as much time as possible with their children, Caroline and John, nicknamed "John-John." "If you bungle raising your children," she said, "I don't think whatever else you do well matters very much." She organized a nursery school inside the White House so the children would have friends their own age; they also had plenty of Kennedy cousins to play with at the family homes in Hyannis Port, Cape Cod, and Palm Beach. Kennedy would read "Snow White" or "Goldilocks and the Three Bears" to them before bed, and they made many cute appearances, horseplaying with

their father for the public. The family zoo included rabbits, lambs, guinea pigs, a pony named Macaroni, a Welsh terrier named Charlie, and Pushinka, the daughter of a Soviet space dog. When her father appeared on the news, Caroline would plant a kiss on the television set. She became a lawyer and author, while John, who grew up to be named *People* magazine's "Sexiest Man Alive," started a political magazine called *George*, in honor of the first president.

Later in his presidency, Kennedy came to respect Jackie as a trusted political confidante and became more involved with their children. He planned to spend his retirement sailing around the Greek Islands, then working in government when one of his brothers, Robert or Edward, became president. But at age forty-six, less than three years into his term, Kennedy was assassinated while riding in an open car in a motorcade. Controversy continues to rage about whether a lone gunman—Lee Harvey Oswald—or a conspiracy was responsible.

Two years after Jackie's death from cancer in 1994, an auction of her estate, including two of Kennedy's rocking chairs, raised more than $30 million.

Lyndon B. Johnson

BORN NEAR JOHNSON CITY, TEXAS, 1908
DIED NEAR SAN ANTONIO, TEXAS, 1973

Teacher, senator, vice president,
then president whose terms were dominated
by the Vietnam War

LYNDON JOHNSON LIVED LARGE. He belched loudly whenever he felt like it, helped himself from other people's plates at banquets, and at dances kissed so many women hello he got lipstick all over his face. A millionaire, he enjoyed scaring guests at his Texas ranch with ninety-mile-an-hour rides in his Lincoln Continental. When relaxed he was an outstanding teller of tall tales, complete with gestures, mimicry, and loud laughter. (He believed a more formal style was required in public, so few witnessed his storytelling skill.) When he visited the pope in Rome, the pope gave him a precious fourteenth-century painting; he gave the pope a picture of Lyndon Johnson.

Johnson *was* large, with protruding ears and a stomach he concealed with a girdle—except when he would lift his shirt to display the scar from his gall bladder surgery. (He did it to reassure people that he wasn't seriously ill, but instead added to his reputation for crudeness.) He loved to eat chipped beef and fresh bread (for breakfast), Texas favorites like chili and barbecued ribs, seafood creole, canned green peas, and lots of gravy. Dieting made him crabby; diet tapioca pudding was the only low-calorie food he enjoyed—several servings of it. If Johnson announced in the morning he was going on a diet, by afternoon the White House would be stocked with cottage cheese, yogurt, melba toast, and diet candy flown in from San Antonio. When the dieting was over, gallons of ice cream and platters of homemade cookies would suddenly reappear. He required an oversize bed to fit his oversize frame, and also a nightly massage.

Johnson's personality could be overbearing, and his temper could be volcanic, especially once he began coming under severe criticism for America's involvement in the Vietnam War. Assistants measured his mood by watching him work and counting the number of points he broke on his highly sharpened pencils. Small things drove him berserk, such as lights left on unnecessarily; he stormed around the White House turning off switches. Demanding of his staff, he would hunt them down in movie theaters, on the golf course, or even in church. Sometimes he degraded people, forcing them to follow him into the bathroom to continue a conversation or to take notes while he brushed his teeth. In the middle of a meeting he'd declare a swimming break and everyone would have to adjourn to the pool, where Johnson swam nude (it saved time) and expected everyone else to do the same. He hand-picked his secretaries, and his chief criterion was appearance ("I can't stand an ugly woman around, or a fat one"). He would reknot a man's tie if he thought it wasn't done right, and he dictated colors and styles for women. At least once he told a senior secretary that all her "girls" needed "more hair spray."

Johnson loved to talk so much that he had phones installed everywhere, including all his cars, boats, planes, and swimming pools (which had special rafts for floating phones). Certain phone lines to his assistants were exclusively his and were marked POTUS (for President of the United States). Woe to someone who didn't pick up a ringing phone promptly—and going to the bathroom was no excuse, as POTUS lines ran there, too. Addicted to news, he held a transistor radio to his ear wherever he walked. In his bedroom and office he had three television screens so he could watch the evening news on all the networks at once. "I seldom think of politics more than eighteen hours a day," he said.

When Johnson proposed to Claudia Taylor on the day of their first date, she thought he was joking—but accepted seven weeks later. A successful businesswoman, known as Lady Bird since childhood, she saw her primary job as creating "a zone of peace, of comfort" around Johnson. He would issue orders and criticize her clothes in front of others, but also hugged and kissed her in public and called her "the most interesting woman I know." She gave him advice on almost every issue, especially anything to do with women's rights. In the White House they slept in a big four-poster bed; he couldn't stand to sleep apart from her. He was close to his two daughters, Lynda Bird and Luci Baines (he liked all family members to have the same initials—their first dog was named Little Beagle), and his grandchildren. Whenever he returned to the White House, Johnson wanted his dogs to run out to greet him, and he kept candy-coated vitamins in his desk drawer to dole out to them. He received some of his harshest criticism, however, when he was photographed picking up his two beagles, Him and Her, by the ears.

He had a bigger budget for gifts than any other president and gave out bracelets, lighters, cuff links, electric toothbrushes (so friends would think of him when they brushed each morning and night), waterproof watches, and orange-and-yellow scarves with 526 "LBJ"s worked into the border. To his staff he gave care packages of his own favorite things—slabs of peanut brittle, fudge cake, six pounds of chocolate. While fierce and ruthless in public, Johnson seemed "warm and mellow" and "gentle, extremely loving" to friends and neighbors. He sincerely wanted to help the poor and disadvantaged, and it saddened him when the war made him extremely unpopular with those who chanted outside his windows, "Hey, hey, LBJ, how many kids did you kill today?" He sometimes lay in bed with the covers pulled up to his chin, blinds drawn, afraid to get up: "I just don't understand those young people," he said once. "Don't they realize I'm really one of them?" He belonged to the Disciples of Christ Church but worshiped at churches of various denominations, and during the war began going to Catholic Mass to pray frequently.

After his presidency, Johnson withdrew from public life to write his memoirs and take care of his ranch. Twenty years earlier a severe heart attack had forced him to quit a three-pack-a-day smoking habit and to begin walking one mile a day. After his third attack, he died, at age sixty-four, leaving a $20-million estate to his daughters. The Vietnam War cease-fire agreement was signed just a few days later.

Richard M. Nixon

BORN IN YORBA LINDA, CALIFORNIA, 1913
DIED IN NEW YORK CITY, 1994

*One of the youngest senators in history,
vice president, and the only president
to resign in disgrace*

RICHARD NIXON'S MOTHER thought he might become a Quaker missionary. Every morning before school he washed produce for the family business, Nixon's Market. When he was seven, the death of a brother affected him deeply, and he determined to make up the loss to his parents by becoming successful. In college he described himself as "the nuttiest of the nutty Nixons . . . doesn't smoke, he drinks very little, he swears less, and he is as crazy as ever. He still thinks an awful lot of his mother."

Finding success as a career politician did not appear to be the obvious choice. Few considered Nixon good-looking, with his smile that never seemed sincere and wavy hair made more curly by the oily hair products he used. He never seemed to relax, was awkward at small talk, and clearly preferred solitude. Those who tagged him "Tricky Dick" for his calculating tactics thought he was a compulsive liar, or at best a chameleon. He had a bitter streak that came out strikingly after he lost a race for governor: "You won't have Nixon to kick around anymore," he announced, meaning that people would miss him now that he was quitting politics.

He didn't quit—and seven years later was possibly our most insecure president, with no apparent sense of humor, a fear of appearing soft or dependent, and a buttoned-up, suspicious manner. To preserve his doings for posterity, he installed an elaborate taping system throughout the government offices. During spells of insomnia he made phone calls to friends and staff—fifty-one calls one night—and was known to wander outside the White House. He worked hunched over yellow legal pads (and got regular back massages from an osteopath). He spent many hours just thinking; one aide said he was "like a cow" chewing "his cud over and over."

Nixon proposed to schoolteacher Thelma Ryan, known as Pat, the night they met; both were acting in a play called *The Dark Tower*. "I thought he was nuts," she said later—she sometimes pretended not to be at home when he stopped by. She finally accepted two years later. Lively in private—they teased and laughed and exchanged mushy love letters—she seemed robotlike in public and was nicknamed "Plastic Pat." She detested political life so much that she obtained from her husband at least four promises (which he broke) that he wouldn't run for office again. They had separate bedrooms and were not openly affectionate. "I certainly am not the Romeo type," Nixon said. Always loyal, she was never angry in public and promoted women's causes when she could. He thought that there would be a woman president in the next fifty years—though he disapproved whenever Pat wore pants.

He was an attentive grandfather to the children of his two daughters, Tricia and Julie (Julie married Eisenhower's grandson David), making time for trips to the circus and historical sites. Awkward even around pets, Nixon would get tangled in the leash when he tried to walk the family dog. One black-and-white spaniel, named Checkers, became the most famous dog in politics when Nixon explained in a speech that he hadn't been using contributions for personal gain. He sarcastically admitted to accepting only one gift—Checkers—that he flat-out refused to return.

Though poor early in his career, Nixon was a sharp-enough poker player to have winnings finance his first campaign; eventually he was a millionaire as a lawyer and author. His best friend was a prosperous Miami businessman, Bebe Rebozo, with whom he vacationed for midnight boating adventures, hours of swimming, dancing (he made progress at the hula), practical jokes, sports talk, and sometimes just silence.

Nixon played popular songs on the piano at parties, enjoyed opera and classical records, and was sometimes heard singing in the shower and yelling his head off at Yankee games. He loved Maryland crab cakes, corned beef hash with egg on top, pineapple rings with cottage cheese, and macadamia nut ice cream. For snacks, he set out silver dishes of miniature Hershey and Baby Ruth candy bars. He regarded his Quaker religion as private and was embarrassed to have people find out he prayed on his knees every night before bed. He was the first president to visit all fifty states, and also China, where, standing atop the famed Great Wall, he said, "I think you would

have to conclude that this is a great wall." The Chinese government gave the United States the most celebrated gift of wild animals from one country to another: two rare giant pandas, Ling-Ling and Hsing-Hsing.

Nixon's downfall began when five agents of CREEP (the Committee to Re-elect the President) were arrested while burglarizing his opponent's Watergate Hotel headquarters. This ignited the worst political scandal in American history, with Nixon forced to resign for attempting to cover up criminal acts. His own taping system trapped him. Notoriously inept with mechanical things, he had the system wired to never shut off—tapes recording misdeeds were used against him. "When the president does it, that means it is not illegal," he said at first, but later admitted, "I let the American people down. And I have to carry that burden with me for the rest of my life."

Nixon was so famous as a non-quitter that many thought he would not survive the first year of his humiliating retirement. He was deeply depressed at first, with more than sixty lawsuits filed against him, but later wrote the best-selling presidential autobiography of this century to pay his expenses. Working from homes in California and New Jersey, he gradually improved his reputation, becoming an unofficial presidential consultant. He read scholarly books on history for hours each night, gave elaborate dinners for intellectuals and old friends, hosted Halloween parties for neighborhood children, and toward the end of his life thought he had achieved the Quaker goal of "peace at the center." He died of a stroke at age eighty-one.

Gerald R. Ford

BORN IN OMAHA, NEBRASKA, 1913

❧

BESIDES RANKING IN THE TOP quarter of his college class, Gerald Ford was such a football star there that two professional teams offered contracts. Instead of accepting, he studied law, worked as a ranger at Yellowstone National Park and as a model (appearing on at least one *Cosmopolitan* magazine cover), and became a congressman. He was appointed vice president, then found himself president after Nixon's resignation, making him our only president who was not elected to either office.

Right-handed when standing up (for sports), Ford was left-handed when sitting (for writing and eating). On his first Sunday as president, he invited photographers over to watch as he slipped off a maroon bathrobe and swam sixteen forty-foot laps, showing off his trim, muscular form. After state dinners, he could stay up until one o'clock in the morning dancing to rock music.

But for someone often deemed our most athletic president, Ford had a reputation as a klutz. After a stumble was captured on film, comedians ridiculed him without mercy. Famously good-humored, Ford laughed along—usually.

He enthusiastically liked everyone, and his first decision as president was to pardon Nixon for any crimes he may have committed. It was the compassionate and healing thing to do, Ford thought, but the move proved unpopular—not that people disliked Ford personally. A few did criticize him as plodding and bland, even saying that he had "spent too much time playing football without a helmet." But others observed, "I never heard him utter an unkind word," "he just doesn't have enemies," and "he's honest, he's decent, and he doesn't have a mean bone in his body."

Wanting a more relaxed White House, Ford asked the Marine band to play the University of Michigan's fight song instead of "Hail to the Chief" at his appearances, and he told Secret Service agents to smile more often. He made a point of saying thank you often to White House staff, and he was the first president to hire someone whose primary job was to write jokes.

Ford's favorite saying was that "eating and sleeping are a waste of time," but he did like to snack on strawberries. Other favorites included stuffed cabbage, navy bean soup, and orange chocolate cake. He smoked a pipe (eight bowls a day) and disliked waste, wearing down pencils to tiny stubs before throwing them away.

In the White House, Ford had more free time to spend with his family than he had earlier as a congressman (when he was on the road, giving up to 230 speeches a year). Elizabeth Bloomer, known as Betty, had wanted to be a famous dancer but became instead an unusually candid First Lady. She publicized her breast cancer in an effort to raise awareness and save lives. She also revealed her substance abuse, later founding the Betty Ford Center for Drug and Alcohol Rehabilitation, where celebrities and the less famous go for help in conquering addictions. "We are the first president and First Lady to share a bedroom in an awfully long time," the Fords announced—their arguments consisted of playful pillow fights. An Episcopalian, Ford would hold hands with Betty in the dark at night as they prayed together.

The four Ford children included a daughter who held her high school prom at the White House, one son who brought rock stars home and admitted publicly that he smoked marijuana, and another who acted on the soap opera *The Young and the Restless*. Of the family pets, Ford's favorite was Liberty, a retriever. Once Ford got locked out of the White House when he took Liberty for a 3:00 A.M. walk, but the dog made up for such inconveniences by providing a diversion whenever Ford felt that meetings were going on too long.

Although lacking obvious enemies, Ford had at least two: Lynette "Squeaky" Fromme (a disciple of mass murderer Charles Manson) and Sara Jane Moore both tried to assassinate him within the same month. He ducked when he saw one gun, and bullets from the other missed him by a few feet. (Since then, presidents are supposed to wear bulletproof vests when they go out in public.)

After failing in his try to become an elected president, Ford retired to a luxurious ranch-style house in Palm Springs, California, to write, speak, and serve on the boards of several corporations.

Jimmy Carter

BORN IN PLAINS, GEORGIA, 1924

*Peanut farmer, governor of Georgia,
and the first man from the Deep South
to become president since the Civil War*

PEOPLE KNEW THEY WERE in for a change from the moment Jimmy and Rosalynn Carter got out of the car during their inaugural parade, holding hands, and walked to the White House. The Carters wanted to promote physical fitness, show confidence in their physical security, and signal that they weren't royalty who had to be chauffeured everywhere. Rosalynn shocked the fashion-conscious by appearing in a previously worn dress at the eleven inaugural parties that night. Carter told the Secret Service agents to stop opening doors for him, ordered all White House thermostats turned down to save energy, and used the stairs (not the elevators) to get around. With a toothy grin and a permanently bent finger from a cotton-gin accident, Carter was unlike any previous president.

His unusual background included studying nuclear physics at the U.S. Naval Academy and then becoming a millionaire from his family-owned peanut business. A Baptist (but not particularly devout until his forties, when he reaffirmed his faith as a born-again Christian), he had a saintly image—humble, compassionate, and quick to forgive. "I have one life and one chance to make it count for something," he said.

He could be moody but rarely expressed anger (and then only by way of an icy stare or a bit of withering sarcasm), and was always willing to admit his own faults. One fault, according to some people, was an obsession with the small details of being president. His earnest ways did not appeal to those who saw them as self-righteous or phony, and he didn't give the impression of having a sense of humor.

Carter dressed simply, preferring his denim farmer clothes; around the White House he wore baggy old cardigans, often with a red tie he considered lucky. He had the music of Bach and Vivaldi piped into his office but also liked Bob Dylan, Paul Simon, and the Allman Brothers. White House cooks fixed Southern food for themselves, so they were happy to make it the official White House diet: grits for breakfast; and for other meals, peanut soup, lentil-and-franks soup, country ham with redeye gravy, corn bread, Georgia peach cobbler, and peanut brittle. Despite all this, Carter lost thirty pounds while in the White House (particularly during his stressful last year, when Iranian militants held fifty-two Americans hostage). He kept on the move by bicycling, playing tennis, skiing, and bowling; on rainy days he jogged up and down stairs. He felt that his life had been affected most deeply by "experiences in wild areas"—especially trout streams all over the country—and was a devoted fisherman.

After marrying Rosalynn Smith—the best friend of his sister (Christian leader Ruth Carter Stapleton)—he taught her to sign her letters to him "I.L.Y.T.G." (I Love You the Goodest). As First Lady she was always a full partner "in every sense of the word," according to Carter, who valued her as "almost a perfect extension of myself." They met on Thursdays for lunch to go over decisions Carter had to make, and the rest of the week he bombarded her with memos scribbled with "Ros, what think?" Openly affectionate, they seemed to have antennae for sensing each other's thoughts. They spoke so alike that some were unnerved—he counted on her to speak for him with authority. "I enjoyed every minute of it," Rosalynn said of her White House time. They took turns reading the Bible to each other in bed; for birthdays he gave her engraved Bible verses. In a famous interview Carter admitted he had been unfaithful to his wife many times—but only "in his heart." ("Jimmy talks too much" was Rosalynn's comment.)

"There is no doubt that the members of my family helped me be a better president," Carter said. He discussed presidential matters with his four children at the supper table and at "family councils." Even Amy, born fifteen years after the youngest of her three brothers, contributed her knowledge of school issues, like how to improve the lunch program. Amy's controversial caretaker was a former prison convict whom Carter believed innocent of the murder for which she'd been convicted (she was later given a full pardon). Amy's brothers worked hard to protect their young sister's privacy. Carter designed a tree house for her within a silver cedar on the White House lawn—her special private place, but also large enough for sleepovers with a few friends. Amy was allowed to come to state dinners, but in case there were boring parts she always brought a book along. In their free time the Carters threw Frisbees on the White House lawn and watched movies—Carter is reported to have seen more movies than any other president, some 465 in four years (preferably rated G and PG).

"President Attacked by Rabbit" read the headlines after a never-explained episode in which Carter, fishing in a pond, had to shoo away with an oar a large rabbit that seemed determined to join him in the boat. The only actual White House pet was Amy's cat, a Siamese named Misty Malarkey Ying Yang. (She tried to add a dog, Grits, who proved too fierce an enemy with the cat.)

Not wanting to be a "frustrated old prune of a man," Carter made himself one of the most active ex-presidents. Accompanied by Rosalynn, he has devoted himself to human rights causes around the world. "If the misery of others leaves you indifferent and with no feeling of sorrow," he said, "then you cannot be called a human being." An advocate for the homeless (and a skilled woodworker), he helps build houses for families in need. Working as a backstage peacemaker, he mediates in international crises and goes on special diplomatic missions for other presidents. His church activities include teaching Sunday school and once a month taking his turn cleaning the churchyard. He also spends hours hiking alone (Rosalynn dislikes hiking) through the two thousand acres of woods he inherited around his hometown of Plains. Wherever he is, he has a laptop computer ready to capture his thoughts. His writings include poetry, a tribute to his adventures hunting and fishing, books for young people, and a presidential diary amounting to five thousand pages in eighteen big black notebooks.

Ronald Reagan

BORN IN TAMPICO, ILLINOIS, 1911

Radio sportscaster, movie actor,
governor of California, and
our oldest president

RONALD REAGAN NEVER lost his glowing tan, from early lifeguard days (he rescued seventy-seven people in all) to the times when he had to work at it. Despite his glamorous look, Hollywood directors said his head seemed too small for his body on camera; to solve the problem, wardrobe designers came up with a style of shirt collar that Reagan wore the rest of his life. On his way to becoming a millionaire movie star, he appeared in some fifty films, including *Knute Rockne—All American, Bedtime for Bonzo* (costarring with a chimpanzee), *A Turkey for President,* and *Kings Row* (featuring one of his most famous lines—"Where's the rest of me?"—spoken when his character wakes up to find his legs have been amputated). He specialized in playing the dependable, wholesome, boy-next-door type. Then a political speech he gave on TV in 1964 drew more contributions than any speech in American history, and within two years he was governor of California.

Reagan went on to become the president thought by many to have the best sense of humor. He flipped to the comics pages first whenever he read newspapers, and he was a gifted storyteller with a perpetual supply of Hollywood anecdotes. He always appeared jolly and optimistic and was hard not to like, even when he said odd things, like "Trees cause more pollution than automobiles." Just a few months into his term, he was seriously wounded by John Hinckley, a mentally disturbed man who believed his actions would win the affection of actress Jodie Foster. Reagan projected not just strength (by walking into the hospital on his own) but also humor: Two hours after surgery to remove the bullet lodged an inch from his heart, he made remarks witty under the circumstances, like "I forgot to duck."

Almost seventy-eight when he left office, Reagan even joked about his age. But he generally appeared vigorous and youthful, denying rumors that he took lots of naps or dyed his hair. He didn't mind admitting to his poor memory, forgetting even the names and faces of White House staff. He was known to doze occasionally at meetings; once in a while he had insomnia, so he'd recite poetry he remembered from childhood until sleep came. Hard of hearing after another actor fired a prop gun close to his head, he had hearing aids in both ears, and he wore contact lenses since the earliest days of their existence. He had little flexibility in one leg after shattering his thigh bone during a charity softball game, and surgery for colon cancer removed two feet of his upper large intestine. Nevertheless, at his mountaintop ranch retreat near Santa Barbara, California, Reagan did his own chores—chopping wood, building fences, and clearing brush. His favorite relaxation was riding: "There's no better place for me to think than on the top of a horse."

Soft-spoken and gentle, Reagan rarely got angry, perhaps throwing a pencil across the room to show it. Few things made him angrier than being accused of racism— equality was one of his core beliefs. A member of the Disciples of Christ Church, he rarely attended services but often expressed deep faith, and he quietly wrote personal checks to people who asked him for help. Hearing his favorite song—"The Battle Hymn of the Republic"—could move him to tears.

Reagan became the only president to have been divorced, a result of ending his first marriage to Jane Wyman, an Oscar-winning actress with whom he had a daughter, Maureen, and adopted a son, Michael. He said his life really began when he met Nancy Davis, another actress, and she echoed the feeling. She quit acting and considered herself the protector of both Reagan's health and place in history. She gave him advice on many issues, though he didn't always take it. Some made fun of the adoring way she stared at him during speeches (calling it "the Look") and how she laughed on cue at jokes she had heard hundreds of times. But she insisted he was her hero, and he claimed to "miss her if she just steps out of the room."

Nancy wore lavish gowns, often in her trademark red, made by America's leading fashion designers. The White House became more formal, with people dressed in white ties and expensive jewelry. The thermostats that had been turned down to save energy during the Carter era were turned back up. The Reagans saw their children—Patti, an actress and writer, and Ronald, a ballet dancer and journalist—and grandchildren at holiday gatherings. A King Charles spaniel named Rex lived in a Cape Cod–style doghouse with red drapes and framed pictures of Reagan and Nancy on the walls.

At five o'clock or so every afternoon Reagan peeled off his clothes, put on swimming trunks, and went to the gym to work out. He described himself as "a popcorn fiend" and thought he could have lived on that alone. More notorious for his tempting jelly-bean jar, he tried to save the coconut ones for himself. He breakfasted on

bran cereal and freshly squeezed orange juice, and his favorite lunch consisted of Mexican food. He and Nancy watched the news or favorite shows while having dinner on TV trays in their bedroom—perhaps macaroni and cheese, hamburger soup, or beef and kidney pie, with apple brown Betty or plum pudding for dessert. He continued to watch movies, current ones at first but later favoring those from his own years in Hollywood.

Presidential security precautions, normally strict, became more so after the assassination attempt. Losing his physical freedom was Reagan's least favorite part of his job. There were few spots where he could take a walk without making himself vulnerable, and even inside the White House, he had to avoid certain windows for fear of shooters. Controversially, Nancy began consulting an astrologer, arranging the president's schedule according to advice about his safety based on the position of stars.

Reagan retired to a luxurious new home in Bel Air, California. In 1994 his Alzheimer's disease became incapacitating, and he released a handwritten farewell letter to the American public, hoping to help others by publicizing the disease.

George Bush

BORN IN MILTON, MASSACHUSETTS, 1924

Navy fighter pilot in World War II,
Texas oilman, director of the Central Intelligence Agency,
vice president, and president

WHY DID GEORGE BUSH sometimes have an image as a wimp? Perhaps because of a childhood nickname ("Fatty McGee McGaw") or because he was born so wealthy that a chauffeur drove him to school and later on dates. Reserved and unfailingly polite, he wanted as president to bring about "a kinder and gentler nation" and didn't see a need for glamour: "I think experience, steadiness, knowing how to interact with people is the way to get things done better." His gestures could be awkward, and though he tried to speak with force (ordering people to "read my lips"), he had a slight lisp and tended to talk rapidly in a high-pitched voice.

But Bush was also a decorated World War II hero, at nineteen one of the youngest combat pilots in the navy. He once spent more than three hours in shark-infested enemy waters after his plane was shot down. While waiting for rescue, with a head wound, being nibbled at by Portuguese men-of-war, he survived by focusing his thoughts on his family, his Episcopalian faith, and (he claimed) the separation of church and state.

Though thin and wiry, left-handed Bush was a versatile athlete, talented enough at baseball to be approached by a professional team while he was in college. He kept his Yale first-baseman's glove in the drawer of his Oval Office desk and rooted for the New York Mets (which were partly owned by his uncle). He jogged three miles a day, insisted on an exercise bike in his hotel suites, pitched horseshoes, traveled annually to Texas to hunt quail, and once personally chased a rat out of the White House pool. He had one scar on his forehead from a soccer accident and another on his hand from a bluefish bite.

Bush drove himself hard until he developed a bleeding ulcer when he was in his thirties, then began balancing work with play. Famously loyal, he maintained wartime and college friendships later in life. He could be flighty, giddy, even prankish—sometimes greeting office visitors by winding up a mechanical bumblebee and letting it buzz around on the floor. Known to choke up with emotion during speech rehearsals, he was able to laugh at himself and was more amused than offended by comedians who mocked his sometimes twisted speech. A friend once described energetic Bush as "popcorn on a hot griddle."

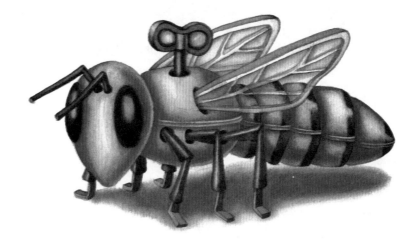

Bush normally didn't pay much attention to other people's clothes, but when he spotted Barbara Pierce's red-and-green dress while at a Christmas dance, he got a friend to introduce them. She dropped out of college to marry him, and throughout their marriage has lived in twenty-nine homes in seventeen cities. On the campaign trail, she took up needlepoint to keep herself awake during speeches she had heard hundreds of times. Once, she got sleepy when a political visitor was talking on and on about Turks, and she prayed that she wouldn't mumble, "Tell me more about the Turds" by mistake.

Barbara called Bush "Poppy" (another childhood nickname), and he called her "Bar." Early on she would playfully deflate his ego in public, but she stopped after he asked her to. She believed that world affairs was a business for men, but freely discussed policy with her husband each morning over Grape-Nuts cereal sprinkled on vanilla yogurt. Sometimes their opinions differed, but she made a point of never dis-agreeing with his views in public. Endearingly unpretentious, seen as "everybody's grandmother," she dressed for comfort, bought sensible dresses off the rack, and wore three strands of fake pearls to hide neck wrinkles. She wanted to age naturally and wouldn't dye her hair (which turned white in her twenties after the death of their three-year-old daughter from leukemia—both Bushes considered the loss the biggest crisis of their marriage).

Both viewed being parents as their "number-one priority"—and the White House was just an extra-comfy family home, with lots of grandchildren, dogs, and warm feelings. The five Bush children all worked for their father in various roles, then went into business or politics. Even during such crises as the Persian Gulf War, Bush stuck to a balance of work and play. He liked action movies, country-and-western music, Broadway show tunes, news and sports on TV, *America's Funniest Home Videos*, and *Murder, She Wrote*. His fondest childhood memories were of family clam-bakes and barbecues at his grandmother's home in Maine, and he eventually bought the house from other relatives and used it as the family's retreat. Though he was down to earth, he never did his own shopping, and some details of ordinary life—such as electronic price scanners at the grocery store—amazed him.

"We must be good to one another" was one of Bush's strongest beliefs, and he at-tended church services regularly, said prayers nightly with Barbara, and read the Bible daily. As a result of one son's severe dyslexia, Barbara became active in pro-moting literacy. She wrote two books from the point of view of the family dogs—*Millie's Book* and *C. Fred's Story*—and donated her profits to literacy organizations. Bush donated the royalties from his autobiography to the United Negro College Fund, of which he was a longtime supporter.

But what was it about broccoli that made Bush hate it so much? He had it banned from the White House: "I'm the president of the United States, and I'm not going to eat any more broccoli!" Nor did he care for most seafood, and though he loved to fish, he gave his catch to Secret Service agents or let it go. He preferred baked stuffed lobster, Chinese food, fried chicken, pork rinds smothered in Tabasco sauce, Mexican food, and peanut butter ice cream.

After his re-election defeat, Bush retired to Houston to play golf, consult, grand-father, and continue to eat what he pleased.

Bill Clinton

BORN IN HOPE, ARKANSAS, 1946

*Law school professor, governor of Arkansas,
and the first president from the post–World War II
"baby boom" generation*

BILL CLINTON MIGHT LIKE this book, as he has been collecting books about the lives of the presidents since childhood. Ten years old when his family got its first television set, he followed the presidential election that year. Seven years later, as a participant in the American Legion's Boys Nation, he shook hands with his idol, President Kennedy. In the 1960s he demonstrated against the Vietnam War and delivered food, with the Red Cross, to burned-out areas of Washington, D.C., after race riots. "I desperately want to make a difference," he said when he reached his ultimate goal: becoming president.

Known for his empathy, Clinton said that he developed "peacemaking skills" as a child from living with his abusive alcoholic stepfather. He is not afraid to show emotion and is often seen misty-eyed in public. Some wonder if his sympathy is phony, but he explains: "I can feel other people's pain a lot more than some people can." He can lose his temper but is usually exuberant and sunny. He has been called the huggiest president in history and has a way of stroking and patting people as he talks to them.

A man of many appetites, Clinton loves to schmooze. He invests such high energy in such a wide variety of topics, from movie critiques to life in the next century, that he has chronic laryngitis (from both voice overuse and allergies). Contact with him can be thrilling (for those exhilarated by his knowledge), exhausting (he once revised a speech so many times that his secretary needed medical treatment), or even

uncomfortable (for those who were dismayed when he answered interview questions about his boxer shorts). Car passengers rarely appreciate his driving, as he talks and gestures more than he watches the road. His unusual ability to argue both sides of an issue has earned him the nickname "Slick Willie" by those who see him as slippery. Giving a short speech is hard—when he gets around to saying "in conclusion," people sometimes break into cheers.

Another love is food—bananas spread with peanut butter, tacos, mango ice cream. Neighbors have seen him demolish an apple in a few bites, core and all, and eat a whole pie without a fork. Plates of nachos or enchiladas disappear instantly, and he seems to inhale chocolate chip cookies. Besides frequenting fast-food places, he likes Southwestern and Italian restaurants and seldom goes to the same eatery twice (for security reasons). He tries to keep his weight down by jogging in the morning, drinking Diet Cokes, and obeying White House chefs (who lifted President Bush's broccoli ban and instead banned creamy desserts—they serve fresh fruit after meals). He is the first president to say in public that he's antismoking.

Clinton loves music—Elvis Presley; the Supremes; Peter, Paul, and Mary; classical (especially Bach); gospel; rock. He plays jazz sax well and doesn't mind showing it off. He spent his fiftieth birthday singing old Beatles songs with friends in Jackson Hole, Wyoming. He loves to read—history, best-sellers, mysteries, even all the books that criticize him. Friday is usually movie night—current ones as well as such classics as *Casablanca* and *High Noon*. He loves card games (particularly hearts played at lightning speed), plays solitaire during late-night calls, and does crosswords in ink at a fast clip. He follows many sports and plays golf several times a month. He sometimes does his own shopping at malls, especially for family gifts.

Clinton bought a brick cottage that Hillary Rodham, a fellow student at Yale Law School, had admired, and presented it to her with his marriage proposal. Later named one of the hundred most influential lawyers in America, Hillary was the family breadwinner, viewed as such an achiever that many hoped she would be the first woman president. Instead, as a major presidential adviser, she continues her work on expanding and enforcing children's rights. She often changes her hairstyle, a lifelong quirk that inspires much talk. While some view her as a humorless and self-righteous policymaker, in private she is mischievous and witty. Intense criticism of the First Lady has been what Clinton deems the most painful part of his presidency. While admitting privately that he has had affairs, he and Hillary have publicly acknowledged commitment to preserving their marriage despite difficulties. Clinton can make fun of his own reputation: "That's a good-looking mummy . . . If I were a single man, I might ask that mummy out," he said when the "Ice Maiden" of prehistoric times was discovered.

Their only child, Chelsea, was so sheltered from the public eye that many didn't know she existed until Clinton ran for president. "She is the most important person in the world to us," her father has said, "and our most important responsibility." They have dinner with her whenever possible and allowed her to choose a church. (Clinton is a Southern Baptist, Hillary a devout Methodist, and Chelsea eventually picked Methodist.) Chelsea loves math and science and dreams of being a doctor or building colonies in space as an astronautical engineer (also an early goal of Hillary's, until NASA wrote her a letter that discouraged women from applying). Clinton is allergic to Chelsea's cat, Socks, who hosts the White House web site for kids on the Internet.

What's left after reaching one's ultimate goal of being elected the president of the United States? For Clinton, that might be returning to the academic world as a university professor or becoming a Supreme Court judge.

At Clinton's rallies, people often hold up signs that say CHELSEA IN 2016.

Selected Bibliography

Aitken, Jonathan. *Nixon, A Life*. Washington, D.C.: Regnery Publishing, 1993.

Ambrose, Stephen E. *Eisenhower: Soldier and President*. New York: Simon & Schuster, 1990.

Boller, Paul F. *Presidential Anecdotes*. New York: Oxford University Press, 1996.

Brookhiser, Richard. *Founding Father: Rediscovering George Washington*. New York: Free Press, 1996.

Burstein, Andrew. *The Inner Jefferson: Portrait of a Grieving Optimist*. Charlottesville: University Press of Virginia, 1995.

Bush, George, with Victor Gold. *Looking Forward: An Autobiography*. New York: Doubleday, 1987.

Califano, Joseph A. *The Triumph & Tragedy of Lyndon Johnson: The White House Years*. New York: Simon & Schuster, 1991.

Carter, Jimmy. *Keeping Faith: Memoirs of a President*. New York: Bantam Books, 1982.

Donald, David Herbert. *Lincoln*. New York: Simon & Schuster, 1995.

Ferling, John E. *John Adams: A Life*. Knoxville: University of Tennessee Press, 1992.

Ford, Gerald R. *A Time to Heal: The Autobiography of Gerald R. Ford*. New York: Harper & Row, 1979.

Goodwin, Doris Kearns. *No Ordinary Time: Franklin and Eleanor Roosevelt: The Home Front in World War II*. New York: Simon & Schuster, 1994.

Heckscher, August. *Woodrow Wilson*. New York: Macmillan, 1991.

Maraniss, David. *First in His Class: A Biography of Bill Clinton*. New York: Simon & Schuster, 1995.

McCullough, David. *Truman*. New York: Simon & Schuster, 1992.

McFeely, William S. *Grant: A Biography*. New York: W. W. Norton, 1981.

Miller, Nathan. *Theodore Roosevelt: A Life*. New York: William Morrow, 1992.

Provensen, Alice. *The Buck Stops Here: The Presidents of the United States*. San Diego: Browndeer Press, Harcourt Brace & Company, 1997.

Reagan, Ronald. *An American Life*. New York: Simon & Schuster, 1990.

Reeves, Richard. *President Kennedy: Profile of Power*. New York: Simon & Schuster, 1993.

Remini, Robert V. *The Life of Andrew Jackson*. New York: Harper & Row, 1988.

Rubel, David. *Scholastic Encyclopedia of the Presidents and Their Times*. New York: Scholastic Reference, 1997.

Rutland, Robert Allen. *James Madison: The Founding Father*. New York: Macmillan, 1987.

Summers, Robert S. "POTUS: Presidents of the United States" (http://www.ipl.org/ref/POTUS/). Internet Public Library, 1997.